D0399331

PRAISE FOR *THE FIRST MILE*

"*The First Mile* is a remarkable gift for anyone who wants to turn small bets into big wins. Scott Anthony shares what he does better than anyone else—combines the best innovation research, consulting experiences, tools, and inspiration into one book."
—Peter Sims, author, *Little Bets: How Breakthrough Ideas Emerge from Small Discoveries*

"Our work with Scott Anthony and Innosight showed us how to transform our organization and seize tomorrow's opportunities. This book provides a road map to turn plans into reality. Required reading for leaders everywhere."
—Gerry Ablaza, CEO and President, Manila Water Company

"Scott Anthony has done it again. Reflecting his unique experience as a consultant, a student, and a practitioner of innovation, *The First Mile* is a valuable and practical guidebook that will help you significantly improve your innovation output."
—Bruce Brown, retired Chief Technology Officer, Procter & Gamble

"If you've ever left a brainstorming meeting frustrated by a lack of follow-through and wondered why it seems so hard to implement good new ideas, or seen promising projects wither away, buy this book. It will transform the way you approach innovation and dramatically enhance your innovation effectiveness."
—Rita Gunther McGrath, Associate Professor, Columbia Business School; author, *The End of Competitive Advantage*

"There are so many unexpected things that can kill promising new ventures, and Scott Anthony has seen them all. In his trademark engaging style, he offers strategies for overcoming these early obstacles and powering through this important stage of innovation. An essential companion for any innovator's journey."
—Keyne Monson, Vice President, Market Development International, Baxter Healthcare

"Humorous, painful, real. Life on the edge includes falling off and learning from the fall. *The First Mile* captures the essence of this concept with advice on how to learn more from each and every fall."
—Karl P. Ronn, Managing Director, Innovation Portfolio Partners

THE FIRST MILE

ALSO BY SCOTT D. ANTHONY

Seeing What's Next: Using the Theories of Innovation to Predict Industry Change, with Clayton M. Christensen and Erik A. Roth

The Innovator's Guide to Growth: Putting Disruptive Innovation to Work, with Mark W. Johnson, Joseph V. Sinfield, and Elizabeth J. Altman

The Silver Lining: An Innovation Playbook for Uncertain Times

Building a Growth Factory, with David Duncan

The Little Black Book of Innovation: How It Works, How to Do It

SCOTT D. ANTHONY

THE FIRST MILE

A LAUNCH MANUAL FOR GETTING GREAT IDEAS INTO THE MARKET

HARVARD BUSINESS REVIEW PRESS
BOSTON, MASSACHUSETTS

Copyright 2014 Harvard Business School Publishing
All rights reserved
Printed in the United States of America

10 9 8 7 6 5 4 3 2 1

No part of this publication may be reproduced, stored in or introduced into a retrieval system, or transmitted, in any form, or by any means (electronic, mechanical, photocopying, recording, or otherwise), without the prior permission of the publisher. Requests for permission should be directed to permissions@hbsp.harvard.edu, or mailed to Permissions, Harvard Business School Publishing, 60 Harvard Way, Boston, Massachusetts 02163.

The web addresses referenced in this book were live and correct at the time of the book's publication but may be subject to change.

Library of Congress Cataloging-in-Publication Data

Anthony, Scott D.
The first mile : a launch manual for getting great ideas into the market / Scott Anthony.
pages cm
Includes bibliographical references.
ISBN 978-1-4221-7176-9 (alk. paper)
1. New products. 2. Technological innovations. I. Title.
HF5415.153.A566 2014
658.5′75—dc23

2013045505

The paper used in this publication meets the requirements of the American National Standard for Permanence of Paper for Publications and Documents in Libraries and Archives Z39.48-1992.

ISBN: 9781422171769
eISBN: 9781625270566

To Joanne, Charlie, Holly, and Harry,
for continuously making the next
mile more fun than the last one.

CONTENTS

PROLOGUE

The Promise and Perils of Innovation's First Mile

It was June 2009. I was in an enclosed space in Bangalore, the IT capital of India, a sprawling metropolis of about 10 million. A stranger who didn't speak English pressed a sharp blade against my neck. And I was loving it.

I was living in what I call the *first mile of innovation*, where you take those precious early steps to translate an idea on paper into an honest-to-goodness business.

The first mile is an exhilarating place.

I was in Bangalore as part of a field visit to determine whether it made strategic sense for me to shift my responsibilities from running Innosight's consulting business to its nascent venture investment and incubation arm. That arm had been set up a few years earlier by Brad Gambill, who had parlayed a small dose of external investment into an interesting portfolio of incubated companies in Singapore, India, and the United States, and a venture capital fund in Singapore with a novel agreement with the government that provided significant leverage. In April 2009, Gambill announced plans to leave Innosight to become the chief strategy officer for LG Electronics.

The company I was visiting was a men's grooming business incubated by Gambill's team under the name Razor Rave. There were a lot of reasons to like the business. The barber market in India was disorganized and had some clear gaps from a customer perspective. There were wonderful high-end salons that catered to wealthy consumers but were too expensive for the mass market. More affordable solutions included not particularly pleasant alternatives, such as individual barber chairs on the side of the road or dingy shops.

A creative, low-cost test run in 2008—involving a rented truck with a barber's chair in the back—increased confidence that the concept resonated with potential customers. The next question was whether Razor Rave could deliver compelling service at a larger scale. So the team (with some support from an outside investor) spent $75,000 to pilot the idea. It built three kiosks, each of which had a single barber chair, deployed them in Bangalore, and carefully monitored progress.

Here are the raw notes from my field visit:

> I visited the Razor Rave stall in Bangalore. A young male consumer was finishing up getting his hair styled. I talked to him afterwards and he said he walked by and was intrigued by the booth. He said

> he found the service to be high value, would return, and would recommend the service to his friends. His male friend had also recently had his hair styled. I received a shave, wash, and had aftershave applied. The 10-minute procedure cost 35 rupees ($0.75). It was a pleasant experience. The stylist clearly didn't speak English, but he was well kempt. The procedure seemed very sanitary, and the inside of the rig was attractive (though there is wasted space). I would personally do the service again, though I have to admit the first two minutes where a strange man had a razor against my throat was a bit scary.

My summary view was that Razor Rave had potential but required significantly more work:

> This is an intriguing concept but far from a business. The team is running multiple experiments around location, service, ambience, and so on. The two critical questions will be building a model that drives high repeat business and attracting, developing, and retaining great franchise owners. These two challenges are clearly interrelated. I think there's a very interesting "there" there, and extra investment might help take this to the next level.

In July 2009, intrigued by what I saw and hungry for a different experience, I officially transitioned over to head up Innosight Ventures and moved out to Singapore. I worked closely with the Razor Rave team to continue to push the idea forward. In January 2010, I sent the following email to one of my colleagues summarizing my excitement about the business:

> There's a lot of hair in India and a legitimate gap in the market.
>
> There is a publicly traded US company that does franchise salons and barbershops (parent of Supercuts) with a $1 billion market capitalization.
>
> Last year Gillette bought The Art of Shaving, demonstrating an interest in service businesses.

Despite my optimism, the reality was that the business was struggling. Upon reflection, the concept we were pushing had a fundamental flaw in its economic model: the single chair. On paper, the kiosk's low overhead made perfect sense, as we could break even by serving only a dozen or so customers a day and could create thousands of Razor Rave franchises across India. However, the reality was that a single-chair model could generate sufficient volume only with a great barber who generated loyal customers and a word-of-mouth following. Once the barber recognized he was the hero of the business, he either demanded high wages or simply left to go to a different shop. And the subscale delivery model couldn't support the wages demanded by a great barber. The so-called hero barber problem sank the business. In April 2010—less than four months after I sent my email—we shut Razor Rave down to focus on other efforts.

The first mile is a perilous place.

Hidden traps snare entrepreneurs, and seemingly never-ending roadblocks slow innovators inside large companies. It's easy to make a wrong turn on the path to the magical combination of a deep customer need, a compelling solution, and a powerful economic model. Creating new things always takes longer and always costs more than you think, making it all too easy to run out of fuel. You can hire the wrong driver, confusing an innovator's personal passion for the commitment and competence required to succeed. When things start going right, you run the risk of accelerating too quickly, leading to a deadly spinout. It's even worse inside a large company, where it's easy to get lost in a dense fog where you study and analyze endlessly, never making particular progress.

These challenges can be overcome. The pages that follow detail a step-by-step guide to speeding through innovation's first mile and describe how to inoculate innovators against some of the first mile's biggest challenges. Let's start by assessing the critical importance of the first mile.

CHAPTER 1

The First Mile Problem

Almost every successful company traces success to a process—sometimes intentional, sometimes accidental—of trial-and-error experimentation that surfaces a winning approach. If you study the history of almost any innovation success story, you find a starting point that bears little resemblance to the finishing point, with interesting twists and turns along the way.

Consider Innosight. The company's first strategy wasn't consulting—it was newsletters. The company's next strategy wasn't consulting—it was developing software that would allow individuals to teach themselves how to get better at innovation. Customers failed to materialize, and Innosight almost ran out of cash. Yet the team persisted, convinced that bringing predictability to innovation was a problem worth solving—even if the initial business model wasn't quite right. Out of necessity, it started running training workshops and doing small consulting projects for companies. In 2003 I started moonlighting with the team, joining officially in August 2003. In 2007—following a business model that bore almost no relation to the original one—revenues crossed $10 million. In the next five years, they would almost triple. Innosight grew from a handful of employees in Woburn, Massachusetts, to a company with seventy-five employees and a presence on three continents.

As the great American philosopher, actor, and occasional boxer Mike Tyson once quipped, "Everybody has a plan, until they get punched in the face." All innovators take their punches; the ones that succeed figure out how to fight back.

For example, a few years ago, two entrepreneurs founded a business called Odeo to help users create and organize podcasts. Notable venture capitalist Charles River Ventures backed the company. One of the founders bought out most of the investors, formed a new company called Obvious, acquired Odeo, and decided to commercialize an internal service that the team had been prototyping to help with internal communication. Seven years later that service—Twitter—had hundreds of millions of users, generated more than $500 million in annual revenue, and was worth an estimated $25 billion after its first day of trading as a public company in November 2013.

Innosight's work building our own business, helping some of the world's leading multinationals create innovative growth businesses, and investing in and incubating start-ups serves as the experience set from which this book offers a solution to a critical problem: successfully creating

INNOVATION DEFINED

Innovation, as used in this book, means *something different that creates value.* The creation of value distinguishes innovation from its typical precursors: invention or creativity. Those are important ingredients, but until an idea meaningfully increases revenue, produces profits, improves the performance of a process, delivers a social benefit, or solves a personal problem, it doesn't qualify as an innovation. The phrase "something different" is intentionally vague. One of the biggest misconceptions people have is that innovation is the job of a select few people—typically white-coated scientists toiling away in a lab, working on a breakthrough technology. That is one way to innovate, but innovation can involve a novel marketing approach, a different pricing model, a new way to organize a team, or even a new way to run a weekly meeting. There are multiple ways to innovate that go way beyond technological breakthroughs. Innovation isn't the job of the few; it is the job of the many.

innovative growth businesses (see "Innovation Defined" for this book's working definition of innovation).

Almost everyone admits that it is a problem, but what is its cause? Senior executives frequently complain that the root problem is a lack of quality ideas, particularly "big ideas." To solve the perceived problem, leaders might run a companywide idea-generation contest, invest in detailed market research, work with an agency that specializes in helping people think "out of the box," or hire someone with the credibility that comes from working at whatever happens to be the hot innovative company of the day.

These all can be useful things to do. But in most cases, they don't solve the real problems that inhibit a company's ability to create growth. Consider the case of a large health care company that spent millions working with an outside consulting company to design a corporatewide idea contest.[1] Two years later, here is how the corporate newsletter described the effort:[2]

> To light a fire, all you need is a spark. That spark is exactly what was produced through the Ideapalooza held in September 2009. Our employees from around the world came together online to share ideas to ignite new innovations for the company. Employees submitted more than 1,000 ideas, ultimately sparking the creation of four internal teams that shaped these ideas into powerful new business concepts.

Sounds exciting, right? But what did those teams accomplish? Read on.

---

1. Truth in advertising—we bid on the project, but lost, largely because we told the client it was working on the wrong problem.

2. Some facts have been disguised in the interest of confidentiality.

> 18 months later the fire still burns. Though we did not directly create the new businesses proposed from the Ideapalooza teams, the business plans helped to inform investments outside our core business. Read on to see the exciting new ways in which we are expanding our business and opening our avenues for growth.

Let's translate that from corporate-speak: "We didn't do anything with the ideas, but thanks for trying!" It's no wonder that employees often react with such cynicism when their leaders announce the latest innovation effort of the day.

It's not just that ideas don't go anywhere. Even those that get commercialized often disappoint. Most executives won't be surprised by analysis by the Nielsen Company that shows that of eleven thousand consumer product launches in North America between 2008 and 2010, only six had first-year sales of more than $25 million, maintained at least 90 percent of sales volume the next year, had faster sales velocity than the category average, and produced cumulative two-year sales that exceeded $200 million. Six. That's 0.05 percent.

The corporate world is drowning in ideas. They think plenty big. But *producing* big—now, there's the clear challenge.

Consider too the fragile nature of start-up companies. Despite the hype that surrounds the precious few success stories, research by Harvard Business School senior lecturer Shikhar Ghosh found that 75 percent of venture capital–backed start-ups—presumably the crème de la crème of the start-up world—failed to return the capital invested in them to their investors (let alone generate positive returns). Of those companies, 95 percent failed to hit the financial milestones laid out in their business plans. Of the more than ten thousand software companies that have received funding from venture capitalists since 2003, only 40 ultimately became worth more than $1 billion. That's 0.4 percent. More generally, the half-life of a new company is about five years. That is, more than 50 percent of companies don't live long enough to blow out six candles on their birthday cake.

Perhaps the root problem is that the world just isn't very good at coming up with innovative ideas. But that neither squares with my firsthand experience with corporate innovators and entrepreneurs, nor is it consistent with the notion that in innovation, the magic isn't in the idea but in the trial-and-error experimentation that so often transforms an idea into a winning business proposition. No one would argue with better ideas, but the core of the problem is a failure in the *first mile*, where an innovator moves an idea from a piece of paper to the market.

The term *first mile* riffs on a term that emerged in the telecommunications industry in the 1990s. Technologies in the "core" of the network were rapidly transforming, but most consumers didn't see much benefit. The problem was that the wires that already ran into people's homes were built for a different kind of traffic. Replacing those wires required heavy investment that could be performed only house by house by an array of construction workers and networking specialists. Pundits termed it the "last mile" problem.

Growth-seeking companies have an interesting inverse to this problem. You give companies a $50 million business and ask them to scale it, and many can do so without batting an eye. You ask them to take a good product and make it better, and they rise to the challenge. But earning the first dollar, euro, or rupee of revenue for a *new* business—particularly one following an unfamiliar business model—is just punishingly difficult. Entrepreneurs get stuck in the first mile too—sometimes they tirelessly pursue an opportunity with fatal flaws or they try so many things that it is hard to figure out what really works.

My view is that the most perilous place for an innovation is in its first mile. I am not the first to make this observation. Thomas Alva Edison is in anyone's innovation hall of fame—after all, the so-called Wizard of Menlo Park gave the world the incandescent lightbulb, the phonograph, the stock ticker tape, and the modern motion picture industry. He clearly wasn't some wild-eyed inventor who came up with impractical ideas. For example, to commercialize the lightbulb, he envisioned and then helped to implement a complete system, including generators, substations, and transmission lines. He designed his lightbulb with an eye to cost-optimizing its operation within this system. He tested the concept in his lab, and then launched a small-scale commercial pilot in lower Manhattan. Others might have nailed the technology, but Edison nailed the business and reaped the rewards. Edison's most famous quote—"Genius is 1 percent inspiration and 99 percent perspiration"—shows a man obsessed with powering through innovation's first mile.[3]

Seventy years after Edison's passing, however, people continue to focus overwhelming energy on the inspiration, and not enough on practical ways to perspire productively.

The Scientific Method and Strategic Uncertainty

In this book, I propose that the fundamental answer to this problem is to apply the scientific method to the management of strategic uncertainty.

You probably remember the scientific method from high school. As defined by the *Oxford English Dictionary*, it is a "method or procedure that has characterized natural science since the 17th century, consisting in systematic observation, measurement, and experiment, and the formulation, testing, and modification of hypotheses."

Cast aside warm memories of Bunsen burners or frog dissections for a minute, and see how the scientific method is popping up in—and transforming—nonobvious places like your kitchen and the baseball diamond.

3. As do other great quotes, such as "If I find 10,000 ways something won't work, I haven't failed. I am not discouraged, because every wrong attempt discarded is often a step forward" and "Opportunity is missed by most people because it is dressed in overalls and looks like work."

The kitchen. It doesn't seem like a place for science. While anyone can become an adequate cook with quality ingredients, the right equipment, a good recipe, and practice, greatness requires artistic flair. Some people have the cooking gene, and some do not. Truly great results come from art, not science. Right?

In 1980, Christopher Kimball decided to take a different approach. What was the optimal way to make scrambled eggs? Bake cookies? Roast a turkey? He and his team would carefully develop a hypothesis, run an experiment, and keep iterating until they got it right. A *New York Times Magazine* profile of Kimball in 2012 described resulting recipes as "worried into technical infallibility after weeks of testing so exacting as to bring an average home cook to the brink of neurasthenia." He created a magazine called *Cook's Illustrated* and a compellingly watchable show called *America's Test Kitchen* to spread the learning to wider audiences. Today, *Cook's Illustrated* has more than 1 million subscribers, its website has more than three hundred thousand paid subscribers, the television show is the highest-rated cooking show on public television, and Kimball has produced a series of cookbooks that users (including one of my brothers) swear by. A recipe doesn't make it into the magazine unless 80 percent of a volunteer army of weekend chefs who try it at home say they would make it again. Kimball fiercely believes that testing leads to the best results and rejects the view that cooking is an art. He told the *Times*, "Cooking isn't creative, and it isn't easy. It's serious, and it's hard to do well, just as everything worth doing is damn hard."

Analysis of baseball has similarly transformed over the past few decades. If you step back to the 1970s, scouts were the lords of the realm. They placed a premium on young players who had the right physical tools over those who produced good results but didn't "look" right. As players developed more of a statistical record, contracts and awards came from excelling in basic statistics, namely batting average, home runs, and runs batted in for hitters, and wins and earned run average for pitchers. Bill James was the spearhead of a movement that transformed performance analysis. He—and other researchers like Craig Wright and Pete Palmer and, more recently, Nate Silver, Voros McCraken, and Tom Tango—approached the sport like a scientist. Baseball, with a huge series of discrete, largely independent events, lends itself to this kind of analysis. Researchers drilled into questions such as: What exactly is it that creates value? Which statistics are most meaningful? Which statistics result primarily from a repeatable skill? Which statistics are heavily influenced by luck or other factors that are hard to repeat? Which in-game strategies actually create value, and which do not? As computing power increased, these researchers could run complex computer simulation models to test their hypotheses. Forward-thinking organizations picked up the research, ran their own experiments, and adjusted strategy based on the data. The so-called Sabermetrics revolution (so named because of the connection to the Society for American Baseball Research, or SABR) crossed into pop culture with the 2003 publication of Michael Lewis's best-seller *Moneyball*, which in 2011 turned into a movie starring Brad Pitt as Oakland Athletics general manager Billy Beane. This revolution has spread to the football field, soccer pitch, and basketball court, changing in-game tactics and contract negotiations.[4]

If the scientific method could transform cooking and sports, why not business and, more specifically, innovations ranging from products and services that power corporate growth to everyday ideas to improve team performance?

Most would argue that science and innovation are at best unrelated and at worst diametrically opposed fields. After all, innovation requires the kind of creativity that people either have or don't have. Creating new businesses requires a master artisan, a splash of randomness, and a dollop of luck.

But just as Kimball changed the way we view cooking and James changed the way we view baseball, research over the past few decades is changing the way the world views innovation. What used to be a dark and mysterious field is becoming increasingly understood and replicable.

Academic work on the management of strategic uncertainty traces back to a seminal 1985 paper by Howard Mintzberg and James Waters called "Of Strategies,

---

4. See, for example, Houston Rockets general manager Daryl Morey's web interview at http://www.reddit.com/r/IAmA/comments/10mrkx/iam_the_houston_rockets_gm_ama/ and the work done by Football Outsiders. Many of the leading thinkers in this field congregate at the annual MIT Sports Analytics conference. See http://www.sloansportsconference.com/.

Deliberate and Emergent." Mintzberg and Waters made the point that, in highly ambiguous circumstances, success typically doesn't come from deliberate planning processes, but from a process of trial-and-error experimentation from which the right strategy would (often unintentionally) emerge. Columbia professor Rita Gunther McGrath and her longtime collaborator Ian MacMillan picked up the thread in a series of writings, including the 1995 *Harvard Business Review* classic "Discovery-Driven Planning" and the 2009 book *Discovery-Driven Growth.*

More recently, Steven Gary Blank has served as the intellectual father of a movement out of Silicon Valley to approach the creation of new companies in more systematic ways. Blank, a serial entrepreneur who now teaches at Stanford and the University of California, Berkeley, notes that a fundamental mistake people make is assuming a start-up is a small version of a big business. It is not. It is a temporary organization in search of a sustainable business model. Blank says that the search must occur in the marketplace, as there are no answers inside the building. Innovators need to bring functional products and services to customers using a process Blank calls *customer discovery.* The foreword of a 2012 book Blank coauthored with entrepreneur Bob Dorf summarized his viewpoint nicely: "*After a half a century* of practice, we know unequivocally that the traditional MBA curriculum for running large companies like IBM, GM, and Boeing does not work in start-ups. In fact, it's toxic . . . The search for a business model requires dramatically different rules, road maps, skill sets, and tools in order to minimize risk and optimize chances for success."

One of Blank's protégés, Eric Ries, introduced thousands of readers to one set of practical tools in his 2011 best-seller *The Lean Startup*. Ries introduced key terms into the innovation lexicon, such as the *minimum viable product* (something of acceptable functionality to attract early customers), the *pivot* (a course correction following in-market learning), *A/B testing* (randomly testing two versions of something like a feature on a website or an advertisement to generate data about consumer preferences), and *build-measure-learn* (a process that follows the precepts of lean manufacturing to reduce waste in start-ups). Innovators, particularly those working on new web-based businesses, embraced the practical toolkit. Finally, Peter Sims provided an inspiring guide for people stuck at the first mile in his 2011 book *Little Bets*, where he described how breakthroughs introduced by comedian Chris Rock, architect Frank Gehry, movie studio Pixar, and many others emerged out of a series of small bets.

Guide to *The First Mile*

Innosight has been working on this topic for more than a decade in three distinct ways:

- **Working alongside clients though innovation's first mile.** Like many consulting companies, Innosight produces its fair share of PowerPoint slides. But consulting teams have also rolled up their sleeves to design and execute in-market experiments in the United States, South Korea, India, China, Australia, the Philippines, and Singapore.

- **Investing and incubating in start-up companies.** Innosight began experimenting with investment and incubation activities by investing in a handful of US start-up companies in 2005. In 2007 those activities merged with emerging incubation activities in Asia under the name Innosight Ventures. From 2007 to 2009, Innosight Ventures raised a small amount of proprietary capital and incubated a dozen businesses in India, Singapore, and the United States. In 2009 it formed the IDEAS Fund, an $8 million fund that is managed in conjunction with the Singapore government as part of the National Framework for Innovation and Enterprise. As of the writing of this book, the IDEAS Fund has invested in eight Singaporean companies (ActSocial, iTwin, Versonic, YFind, Chope, the Luxe Nomad, Referral Candy, and The Mobile Gamer). All told, Innosight has investigated more than four hundred opportunities and participated in operationalizing close to thirty ideas.

- **Creating corporate cultures that support experimentation.** Large organizations by definition are designed

> to execute today's business model, not search for tomorrow's. The pace of change in today's world mandates that companies find a way to balance execution activities and search activities, and do it in a way so that balance comes naturally rather than relying on constant senior leader intervention. Innosight has helped leadership teams around the globe develop systems and structures that support strategic experimentation.

The text that follows summarizes lessons from these experiences. The book's first section builds the First Mile Toolkit, a practical way for teams to speed through innovation's first mile. Specifically, the section walks through a four-part process with the handy acronym DEFT: *document* your idea (chapter 2), *evaluate* it from multiple perspectives to identify uncertainties (chapter 3), *focus* on the most critical ones (chapter 4), and *test* to increase confidence (broken into two chapters: chapter 5 detailing keys to successful test design and execution and chapter 6 presenting a "cookbook" of fourteen specific strategic experiments). The toolkit will help innovators to answer questions such as: How do I reliably identify the weak points in my strategy? What is the difference between a fact and an assumption? What kind of experiments will allow me to learn what I need? How do I manage those experiments?

While describing the process is straightforward, following it is not, particularly inside large organizations. The book's second section describes how to overcome the most common first mile challenges (chapter 7), explores systems that organizations can build to make experimentation come more naturally (chapter 8), and provides pointers for leaders seeking to develop their ability to handle the uncertainty that characterizes the first mile—and the broader strategic challenges facing leaders in the coming age of discontinuity (chapter 9).

While there are a few "classic" examples, the book seeks as much as possible to detail lesser-known case studies, such as an effort to build a disruptive audio console, a word-of-mouth marketing start-up trying to break through in China, Kraft's foray into the pizza truck business, and Innosight's own efforts to develop new offerings and business models.

This book is primarily targeted at managers inside companies tasked with developing and commercializing new ideas and leaders looking to improve their ability to govern in today's turbulent times. But it holds lessons for anyone who is venturing into the unknown, be it entrepreneurs trying to determine if it is worth going all-in on their ideas or even parents trying to figure out how to potty train their child—anyone who has an idea that, like all ideas, is partially right and partially wrong. How do you move from the sketch pad to the market, or equivalent? The road ahead is littered with hidden traps and powerful roadblocks, many of which we've painfully encountered in our own field experience. Read on to learn more.

Key Messages from This Chapter

1. Innovation's first mile is fraught with difficulties.
2. The scientific management of strategic uncertainty is the key to overcoming these difficulties.
3. This book will augment tools provided by the *lean start-up* movement based on Innosight's experience consulting to large companies and incubating and investing in start-ups.

PART I

The First Mile Toolkit

The following chapters build the First Mile Toolkit—a four-step process to manage strategic uncertainty. The chapters that follow describe how to:

- Document an idea to help surface hidden assumptions
- Evaluate that idea from multiple angles
- Focus on the most critical strategic uncertainties
- Test rigorously and adapt quickly

The acronym DEFT serves as an apt reminder that you'll need to be adroit at handling the unpredictable twists and turns the first mile often involves, which makes a rigorous process that much more important.

CHAPTER 2

Document What You Plan to Do

The first stage in the DEFT process—*document* your idea—sounds innocent enough: write down what it is you are actually hoping to do. Amazingly enough, however, it is a step many innovators miss. As an example, our investment unit has reviewed close to four hundred plans over the past few years. Most of those plans deeply describe a cool technology *or* a massive market opportunity. Only a subset covers both. An even smaller number also describes the idea's economics. Ever fewer talk about nitty-gritty operational details.

Adherents of the lean start-up methodology sometimes take the extreme perspective that research and thinking are useless—that learning comes only from developing prototypes and testing in-market. That's not right. Any initial strategy for a new growth business will be partially wrong, but the thinking that went into it is likely to be partially right too. Consider the research Jeff Bezos did before he founded Amazon.com, which led him to focus on books rather than on music, clothing, or electronic appliances. Studying the book market then led Bezos to locate his company near some of the major book distributors in the Northwest of the United States. Sure, he might have gotten there through experimentation, but studying market dynamics helped him to cut a couple of corners. There's no doubt that people inside large companies can over-engineer business plans, but don't let the pendulum swing too far the other way. Good innovators invest the time to research their opportunities and formulate the most robust hypotheses they can so that they focus experiments on areas where the learning will have the greatest impact.

Because there isn't one best way to document an idea, this chapter lays out a few different approaches to consider. It also describes a few tools that can help with documentation and highlights the most common mistakes innovators make.

A Starting Point: The First Mile Trinity

What does it take to successfully do something different that creates value? At the simplest level, any successful innovations share three characteristics:

- It must address a legitimate market or customer need ("Is there a need?" or in plain language "Who cares?").

- It must address that need in a reliable and compelling way ("Can we do it?" or "Can we deliver?").
- It must successfully create value along whatever metrics are pertinent for a particular effort ("Do the numbers work?" or "Does it matter?").

So, at a basic level, you should be able to describe the specific problem you are targeting, the way in which you will address that problem (both in the short term and in the long term), and how that solution will translate into meaningful impact along whatever dimensions matter to you (revenue, profits, cash flow, process improvement, and so on).

The Next Step: Twenty-Seven Innovation Questions

While those three areas seem straightforward, providing good answers requires more detailed thinking. For example, to explain the nature of the need for your innovation, you have to understand who are the actual customers or end users and who influences them. You need to know how and why customers will use your idea and stakeholders will support it. Determining the viability of an idea requires thinking through elements such as production and distribution, and competitive response as well. Understanding whether it matters requires developing detailed understanding of how revenues are earned, what costs are required, and the flow of cash in the business.

So, a second-order description of an idea should consider (at least) twenty-seven specific questions that good innovators should be able to answer:

THE TARGET CUSTOMER

1. Who is the customer (or customers, if it is a multi-sided business like a media business that attracts an audience of consumers and then sells advertising to companies hoping to reach those consumers)?
2. What job is the customer struggling to get done?[1]
3. What suggests that the job is important and unsatisfied?

KEY STAKEHOLDERS

4. Who else is involved in the decision to purchase and use an offering?
5. What are their jobs to be done?
6. Why will they support the idea?

---

1. The term *job* appears in other works by Innosight and Clayton Christensen. The basic notion is to understand the true motivator of purchase and use, which is customers having a problem that they can't adequately address on their own. When customers encounter one of these jobs, they "hire" a product or service to get it done.

THE IDEA

7. What is the essence of the idea?
8. How will the idea ease the pain of the customers and key stakeholders?
9. How does it compare with other ways the customers could get the job done?
10. What makes it different and better?
11. What will it look and feel like?

THE ECONOMICS

12. What are the most likely revenue streams?
13. What is the cost of earning those revenues?
14. What infrastructure will be required?
15. What capital expenditures are required?

THE COMMERCIALIZATION PATH

16. What is the foothold market where you will start?
17. What is the plan to expand from the foothold?
18. Which competitive solutions are you most worried about? How will you beat them? How might you get them to ignore you?

OPERATIONS

19. What are the key activities involved in the opportunity?

20. Who is doing what?

21. What will you do?

22. What partnerships will you need to form?

23. What will you need to acquire?

THE TEAM

24. Who is on the team?

25. What have they done in the past that suggests that they have any chance of succeeding?

THE FINANCING

26. How much money is required to execute the plan?

27. How long will it take to earn a return on that money?

Obviously, some of these questions are easier to answer than others—and that's okay. Part of the value of documenting is to get a better sense of what you actually *know* as opposed to what you are assuming. Documenting assumptions also makes it easier to revise a plan if basic assumptions change in the market. If you are working on a team, answer these questions as a group. Even people who work together on a daily basis frequently have differing underlying assumptions about an idea.

Capture Tools

There are three tools that we've found helpful to document a concept.

The first is something we call an *idea resume.* Just like a person's resume condenses his or her professional history to one to two pages, an idea resume captures all of the salient components of an idea on a single page. We introduced the concept in our 2008 book, *The Innovator's Guide to Growth*, and continue to believe in the usefulness of writing down the key elements of an idea. Fitting an idea on a page means making choices about which elements to include—a typical "vertical" idea resume on Microsoft Word has ten to twelve factors. A PowerPoint slide might have only four or five elements. Ideally, an idea resume should have more than just words—it should have a visual depiction (that's a fancy way to say a drawing) of the idea. Figure 2-1 shows one version of a blank idea resume (note, some of the concepts here, such as the calculation of impact, critical uncertainties, and testing plan, are covered in more depth in subsequent chapters). A blank version of this tool can be downloaded from the companion website to this book.

Another popular tool is the *business model canvas*, described in detail in the international best-seller *Business Model Generation*, by Alexander Osterwalder and Yves

FIGURE 2-1

The idea resume

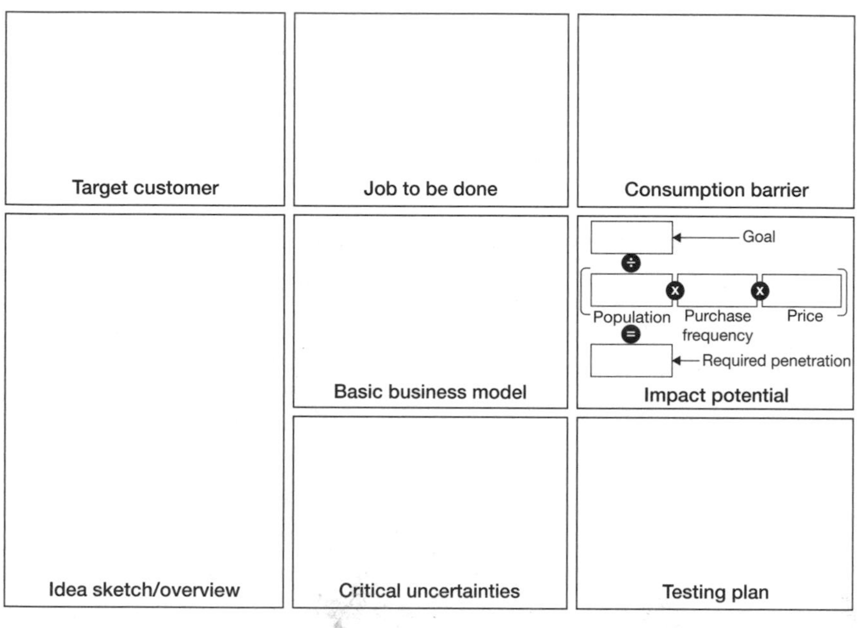

Pigneur. The tool's simplicity and visual clarity has made it a go-to source for many innovators. The canvas captures on a single page key elements of the business model—namely the customer, the offering, the channel to market, the marketing approach, and more. To capitalize on the tool's popularity, Osterwalder has built a set of capture tools that work on laptops and tablets like the Apple iPad; these are available at Osterwalder's website (www.businessmodelalchemist.com).

The third approach is to create a so-called business plan. Our bias is to avoid overly dense one hundred–plus page documents covering every conceivable component of an idea.[2] Since every idea is partially right and partially wrong, obsessing about perfectly polished business plans is a waste of time. Rather, innovators should spend just enough time to make sure they have captured the essence of their idea so they can easily share it with others and move on to the next steps of the First Mile Toolkit.

Our venture capital arm has reviewed hundreds of business plans. One memorable one was the pitch for Wildfire in 2010. The idea was to develop a systematic approach to word-of-mouth marketing in China. There was a clearly demonstrated market need—a lack of media inventory made traditional advertising vehicles (thirty-second television commercials, newspaper advertisements, and the like) very expensive. To get their messages out, companies would blanket a city with leaflets or invest in in-store promoters who would push products. Further, global research consistently shows that recommendations from trusted sources carry significantly more weight than mass-market advertising messages. The strong social norms around *guanxi*, which essentially describes the power of trust-based relationships between people, makes China an even better market for word-of-mouth marketing.

Wildfire's founding team met while studying at INSEAD's campus in Singapore. Benjamin Duvall had previously worked at BzzAgent, a company that developed a word-of-mouth marketing business in the United

2. Of course, make sure you know your audience. Technically minded reviewers might demand density, and certain venture capital investors will too.

States, and spoke fluent Chinese. His cofounder, Christoph Zrenner, had developed software that could help manage the myriad details that would form the backbone of the business.[3]

The core of Wildfire's document was all of fourteen pages long, organized around ten unique aspects of Wildfire. Table 2-1 details those areas and evaluates how correct the team's assertions were.

Wildfire (which rebranded itself ActSocial in early 2014), got some things right but had some significant misses as well. That's normal. The comprehensive nature of the plan made it clear that the team had thought about their business, increasing our confidence in making an investment. It also was a nice blend of strategic thinking, analytics, and visual descriptions. The plan is available at a companion website to this book.

When we work with corporations, we typically use a mini business plan that bears strong similarities to Wildfire's plan. While the nature of each plan is very client specific, the table of contents generally includes:

- An executive summary
- The target consumers and their problem
- The proposed solution (including a sketch or a picture of an early prototype)

3. The software was first developed to help manage the ratings students gave teachers after classes. Zrenner then explored using the same system to manage pharmaceutical drug trials before landing on word-of-mouth marketing.

TABLE 2-1

Overview of Wildfire's business plan

Area	Wildfire 2010 assertion	What it meant	Late-2013 view
Pain	Marketers are desperate to break out of the arms race in Asia-Pacific and China.	Limited traditional media (TV commercials, newspaper ads) meant rapidly escalating costs.	Market interest in novel solutions in Asia Pacific has been consistently high.
Solution	A set of eight proprietary tools that successfully solve a significant problem for marketers	Specific mechanisms to form, activate, and monitor a network of influencers	The envisioned solution was mostly "offline," involving human-to-human interactions. The solution that emerged was a blend of offline and online tools that could monitor and influence people using social networks.
Traction	Two Fortune 500 anchor clients and three smaller accounts within first year in business	Early interest from big companies suggested an interesting opportunity to scale.	The early services model had a longer-than-anticipated sales cycle, so real traction took longer to develop.
Market	Large and rapidly growing market	A variety of analysts suggested that advertising in China generally and word-of-mouth marketing specifically would grow substantially.	Specific projections are always wrong, but the market certainly has grown over the past few years.
Positioning	An innovative "blue ocean" proposition	Wildfire was trying to compete in very different ways from traditional promotional vehicles.	Word-of-mouth marketing has maintained a unique position compared with traditional offerings, but hybrid solutions combining word-of-mouth and traditional means are emerging.

(continued)

TABLE 2-1 *(continued)*

Area	Wildfire 2010 assertion	What it meant	Late-2013 view
Revenue model	Defensible, profitable, and scalable business model	The team projected that a company would spend $2 million on a single program, which made the business very attractive.	Prices were lower than expected, and sales took much longer to close, which drove important business model modifications.
Barriers	The first to adapt influencer marketing for the Asian market and in a strong competitive situation	Wildfire believed that its unique approach and early traction would ward off competitors.	Global competitors have been slow to enter the market, but Wildfire has had to contend with a range of start-ups.
Status	We have a plan.	The team had clear short- and medium-term milestones.	They did some parts of the plan and not others, hit some milestones and not others.
Team	A highly effective and localized team with a proven track record	Wildfire had all key leadership positions filled with people with interesting, complementary backgrounds.	By 2012 it was clear the team lacked top-flight sales and market development capabilities, leading to it bringing in new key executives.
Financials	Wildfire has proven the business, demonstrated profitability, and is ready for next-round funding.	Wildfire projected that it could be sold as soon as 2011 or issue stock to the public in 2014.	It always takes longer—and it always costs more. Wildfire learned that lesson.

- Key business model elements
- Plan to scale the idea
- Thumbnail financials (see chapter 3 for suggested approaches)
- Critical assumptions
- Proposed testing plan

You can download a blank business plan template and an example for the Kraft pizza truck (discussed in chapter 6) at innovationsfirstmile.com.

Four Watch-Outs

It takes diligence and discipline to document an idea. No matter what approach you follow, watch out for these four common mistakes.

1. Confusing a Concept and a Business

Many innovation efforts start with a simple question. "What if we . . ." often starts the question. "What if we brought word-of-mouth marketing to China?" asked Wildfire. "What if I could use the internet to sell books at low price points?" Jeff Bezos wondered. "What if we could rid the word of malaria?" Bill Gates asked when he set up his foundation. A fragment of an idea is a great starting point but an insufficient ending point. Assuming your intent is to start a business or create new growth inside an existing business, the reason you are innovating is ultimately to create revenue that translates into profits that translate into free cash flow. And you can't dream of revenues, profits, and cash flow unless you solve operational issues such as production, distribution, postsales support, and so on. Financial and operational issues can be intimidating to innovators who lack training in how to read financial statements or design and manage a supply chain. Fortunately, a number of readily accessible tools can demystify the jargon that makes it seem like Wall Street analysts are speaking a different language. I particularly recommend Bob Higgins's *Analysis for Financial Management* as a way to get a good understanding of basic financial terms and techniques.

2. Focusing Only on the Beginning or the End

Some innovators paint exciting visions of what the future could hold; others describe in very precise detail what they will do in the very near term. The best innovators, however, can do both. It is important to have precision about what is coming next. Lofty plans often never get realized. And since those plans aren't quite right anyway, a crisp starting point helps to make sure the process of trial-and-error experimentation to find the right strategy leaves the starting blocks. Innovators should be able to explain with some degree of precision what will happen in the next thirty, ninety, and 360 days. One useful technique to really bring an idea to life is to envision how the company will earn its first dollar of revenue. Who specifically will be the customer? What will that customer be paying for? How will he or she get it? At the same time, it is important to have some kind of viewpoint for what the ultimate destination could be (while recognizing that vision could be 100 percent wrong). Innovators should be adept at painting a picture of what the world could look like in three to five years if they are successful. Both frames are important.

3. Looking from the Perspective of a Single Set of Stakeholders

The world is a complicated place. Think about all of the people who might touch a new treatment mechanism for diabetes that integrates monitoring technology and a smartphone application that supports regular exercise and healthy eating. There is, of course, the patient who ultimately receives the treatment. A spouse, friends, and families can influence the patient's decision to try to stick to a new regimen. Writers for technology blogs could influence the patient too. A general practitioner or specialist doctor might have to prescribe the product. A hospital administrator has to approve its use. An insurance company executive or government payer might determine reimbursement terms. A regulator could approve use, or not. If a thread in this complicated web breaks, the chances for ultimate success decrease substantially. Not every business is as complicated as health care, but a good description of an idea highlights why it makes sense for all relevant stakeholders.

4. Getting the Head but Not the Heart

Which do you find more compelling? A newspaper story describing the basic plot of a film, or a sixty-second video? If a picture is worth a thousand words, a good sixty-second video is worth a book. Too many innovators try to pound people into submission through litanies of facts and figures. Please make sure to do your homework and think as comprehensively as you can about your idea. But remember—if you *only* win the head but *don't* win the heart, you've lost the battle.

Start by thinking about telling a story about your idea. As an innovator typically needs to engage with a range of different stakeholders, a well-crafted story can be a captivating way to get people's attention. Use complete sentences and paragraphs as part of the story—bullet points can be superficial or open to subjective interpretation. Support your story with visual elements. Create a simple video. Develop a mock magazine advertisement. Build a fake website. Create a storyboard, a six-frame cartoon that shows how consumers will experience your idea. Are these solutions beyond your expertise? Go to Elance.com and find some low-cost help. Read books on the subject, like Nancy Duarte's *Resonate*.

Find a way to make your idea tangible. Consider how Dorothea Koh helped a medical device company at which she worked to come up with a new way to teach diabetic consumers how to use the company's insulin pump. An insulin pump provides a continuous flow of insulin through

A prototype of Dorothea Koh's wearable skin

a tube that a consumer inserts into his abdomen. Historically, a company representative would demonstrate how to insert the tube using a plastic mold about the size of a large hardcover book. The user would sit at a table and insert the tube into the mold. Of course, those actions only roughly approximated what the consumer would have to do to insert the tube into her own abdomen; kinesthetically, it is vastly different to put a tube into a mold on a table than to insert a tube into your body. What if, Koh thought, the company created "wearable skin" so consumers got a better sense as to how to insert the tube? Instead of creating a detailed PowerPoint presentation, Koh spent all of five minutes and less than $1 to create a prototype. Management embraced the idea, and the company started rolling it out in 2012.

Innovation is hard work, and it is tempting to jump as quickly as possible to execution. The effort to document an idea is worth it, however, as it facilitates and amplifies the impact of subsequent stages of the process. Chapter 3 describes how to evaluate an idea to begin to understand its strengths, weaknesses, and key uncertainties.

Key Messages from This Chapter

1. It is important to rigorously document an idea to begin to understand critical assumptions.
2. Make sure you cover multiple angles, notably the market opportunity, the specific idea, and how that idea will create value.
3. Don't spend too much time documenting, because your idea is going to change.

CHAPTER 3

Evaluate

After documenting an idea, the next step is to evaluate it. The point here isn't to make a final decision about whether to proceed. Rather, following this chapter's guidance helps to highlight the uncertainties underpinning an idea. Chapter 4 will then describe how to pick out the uncertainties that require the most time and attention. If you are working on a specific idea, make sure you start this chapter with a pen and paper or other note-taking mechanism in hand so that you can immediately begin jotting down strategic uncertainties. Also keep your eyes open for immediate opportunities to refine and strengthen your idea. Thoroughly examining an idea actually serves as a low-risk way to test how well it holds together!

Before you begin using the evaluation mechanisms described in this chapter, make sure you are clear about the strategic intent behind your innovation effort. Put another way—what, precisely, are you trying to accomplish? It could be one or more of the items on the list below:

- Grow top-line revenue
- Create free cash flow
- Increase employee morale and retention
- Build market share
- Improve the perception of a brand
- Strengthen the performance of a process
- Solve a specific problem
- Positively impact the world

Beyond the "what," make sure you have clarity about "how" you will measure success, ideally with some degree of precision. If financial returns are the ultimate target, try to have good answers to questions such as: What are the ultimate revenue targets? By when? What do operating margins have to be? How much investment will be tolerated? As described in "Assert the Answer," our general bias, particularly in the early stage of innovation, is to pick a desired outcome and focus on the assumptions that would need to be true for that outcome to be plausible rather than to obsess about the answer itself.

With the "what" and "how" codified, consider three categories of evaluation: pattern-based qualitative analysis to highlight strategic uncertainties, financial analysis to zero in on business model and operational uncertainties, and role-playing to identify other weak links.

ASSERT THE ANSWER

One of the silliest dances done in corporations is the one between a project review committee and a project team. The team dutifully creates a spreadsheet with their best estimates of an idea's potential. They show the results to their review committee. The numbers are okay, but too small to get anyone excited. So they send the team back. Magically, the team comes back with a new set of assumptions that are bigger, but not so big that they seem unbelievable. Did the team suddenly develop new knowledge that pushed assumptions up? Nope. In many cases, one person on the team was sophisticated enough with Microsoft Excel to use a function called "goal seek" to determine precisely what they had to assume to get above a threshold. This is just silly. Instead, start any financial effort by asserting a minimally acceptable answer. That answer can be revenues, profits, an efficiency boost, or something else entirely. But the focus of all subsequent activities isn't to build *up* to an answer; it's to work *down* to identify the most critical unknowns.

Pattern-Based Analysis

Ted Williams was one of the greatest baseball hitters that ever lived. His lifetime 0.344 batting average is the seventh-highest of all time, and the highest of any player born after 1900. Williams once said, "Baseball is the only field of endeavor where a man can succeed three times out of ten and be considered a good performer." The reality is that kind of success can characterize any activity where luck and skill combine to determine outcomes (Michael Mauboussin has studied this in more depth; see chapter 8 for more), including, of course, innovation. In those activities, understanding the patterns and processes that characterize success provides reasonable gauges to judge long-term potential without detailed data.

In the case of innovation, that means evaluating uncertain innovation strategies against patterns that connect historically successful strategies. This process involves a large amount of subjective judgment—would that there were a comprehensive ISO 9001 checklist for new business creation that painstakingly laid out the 326 elements that predictably would generate a successful business!

Based on our research and field experience, we've developed a tool that we use in our investment activities to assess ideas (the full tool appears in appendix A). It features eighteen separate areas, with grounded statements to indicate "poor," "average," and "good" fit.

The evaluation starts by looking at the essence of the idea itself. Beyond obvious areas, such as whether there is indeed a market need, a compelling solution to that need, and an attractive economic model, other areas probe whether there is clear starting "foothold," a path to expand from the foothold, and a good plan to mitigate the idea's key risks (a topic discussed in more depth in the following chapters).

The next set of questions evaluates the team. Many venture capitalists will tell you that they would back an A team with a B idea over a B team with an A idea. Academic research actually suggests that the selection of the industry or market space matters more than the team, but it is clear that the quality and experience of the team matter a great deal.

We pay particular attention to two factors related to the team. The first is a team's relevant experience. From 2007 to 2009, Innosight's ventures arm incubated a wide range of business opportunities. Most of that work was done by smart generalists, many of whom had cut their teeth in our consulting business. They would come up with ideas that looked interesting to smart businesspeople who lacked contextual knowledge. For example, one idea was a model to improve agricultural logistics in India. It's a big problem—experts estimate that about a third of fruits and vegetables spoil due to supply chain inefficiencies. However, as the team dug deeper, it began to encounter roadblocks that people with more domain expertise could have anticipated. As one team member said, "Even without our 'brilliant' model, people had figured out a solution to the problem." Another team led by an American and Indonesian attempted to build a distribution business in India. The team was smart and dedicated, but they wasted time and money dealing with challenges that someone with industry and market knowledge would have anticipated. Too much expertise can be a curse, but a choice between someone with specific skills and a generalist who lacks any unique capabilities should be considered carefully.

The second area of importance is having a sufficiently deep team. There is a myth that innovation comes from an individual working by candlelight in a basement or garage. The reality is that successful innovation requires a team with complementary skills. If that team lacks critical mass, the chances of success diminish. (Chapter 7 provides more detail about specific characteristics that indicate that an individual is positioned to excel in the first mile.)

The final set of questions evaluates the path to profits. These questions are particularly important for companies that hope to participate in complicated ecosystems that feature distinct buyers, users, influencers, suppliers, and more. In these circumstances, it is important to make sure that there aren't chokeholds that can stop good ideas. Rod Adner's 2012 book, *The Wide Lens*, provides a range of useful tools to perform more detailed analysis of businesses that compete in these circumstances.

We use the checklist in appendix A whenever we are considering investing in an idea. There's no magic threshold an idea has to cross; the point of the evaluation is to help us determine what needs to be studied more deeply and provide guidance to the management team about where they should focus their next set of activities.

Financial Modeling

Spreadsheet jockeys rejoice! We are finally at the stage of the book where your financial acumen will come in handy.

After all, a very common—and frequently useful—evaluation tool (particularly inside big companies) is detailed financial analysis.

Let's start by praising finance whizzes. If the finance function played a role in a movie about innovation, it would likely be the mustache-twirling, black-clothes-wearing villain. As they lord over the corporate coffers, their demands for compelling proof before they dole out precious dollars (or equivalent) make it next to impossible for uncertain ideas to proceed forward. Scapegoating finance isn't really fair. The finance function accelerates innovation in a number of ways. Parsimonious financial managers are actually one of innovation's best friends. After all, as the old saying goes, "Necessity is the mother of invention." Abundance can curse innovation by slowing it down or making it inflexible. Building detailed financial models also provides a rich vehicle for learning because it forces innovators to answer questions such as:

- How, precisely, will we make money?
- What will be the unit costs involved in a transaction?
- What overheads will be required to build a scale business?
- How will profits translate into free cash flow?

Going through these questions can highlight opportunities for innovative business models, such as new pricing models, financing schemes, or inventory management mechanisms. More often than not, these business model levers are critical components of sustainable businesses. Asking the questions also helps to highlight underlying assumptions that are too easy to gloss over until you build a detailed spreadsheet.

Of course, a dose of caution is needed when building financial models. Intricate spreadsheets to support an idea can provide great insight but can take significant amount of effort to construct. And it's too easy to get lost within the bowels of a complicated spreadsheet. The statistician George E. P. Box once wrote, "All models are wrong, but some models are useful." Since your financial model is replete with assumptions, seek to make it as simple as possible. Many a corporate innovator has spent hours perfecting a spreadsheet only to get deluged by questions that require substantial analysis and rework. The truth is, the spreadsheet for a truly novel idea is largely made up anyway.

Scott Cook is the chairman and cofounder of the software company Intuit, a multibillion-dollar company that sells Quicken, QuickBooks, TurboTax, and a range of other solutions. The company regularly ranks as one of the world's most innovative. What does a billionaire who made his fortune bringing discipline to individual and small business financial management say about the value of spreadsheets in innovation?

"We tell our disruptive teams to not do volume forecasts," Cook says. "Do not do a spreadsheet with volume forecasts on it, because it is unforecastable. You really cannot know. So why waste the time doing bogus numbers that are unknowable? The finance department may ask for them, so spend five minutes, do something quickly, but the leadership should not focus on those numbers. They are wrong, you just don't know in what direction."

Again—this is a guy who has made all of his money selling software to help people and businesses manage their finances telling people to *not do financial forecasts*! Cook's perspective is extreme, and perhaps even dangerous if you are an entrepreneur looking to raise capital from financially sophisticated investors, but it is instructive. One reason Cook suggests people spend so little time on the numbers is his own experience. In a memorable 2006 *BusinessWeek* article, he quipped, "For every one of our failures we had spreadsheets that looked awesome." Unfortunately, you can't cash an awesome spreadsheet. So make sure that your financial analysis focuses more on unearthing and documenting key assumptions than on driving toward an answer that represents nothing more than the mathematical relationship between made-up numbers.

Also remember that a company's business model is often imprinted in its financial tools. If you work for a big company and you use a prepopulated template, there could be dozens of hidden assumptions that make perfect sense for the base business but could cause problems for new businesses. For example, a few years ago a well-known consumer packaged goods company introduced a high-priced device. The financial forecasts looked great. But when the company started selling the device, it encountered a problem. When customers buy a tube of toothpaste but decide they don't like the taste, they throw it in the trash. When customers buy a $200 device and decide they don't like it, a significant portion will return it. The company's model implicitly assumed almost no returns—and when that assumption proved false . . .

With these caveats in hand, the text that follows details four financial techniques that can bring clarity to an idea's most critical uncertainties. They range from simple calculations that can be done in less than an hour to more sophisticated techniques that require specialized (but not difficult to use) software programs. The companion website for this book contains templates to help with the analyses described below.

1. Calculate Your Idea's 4P's

The first technique involves developing a model that will fit on the back of an envelope or a cocktail napkin. I am partial to what I call a *4P calculation*—a quick calculation that combines the target *population*, planned *pricing*, expected *purchase frequency*, and required *penetration* to achieve an identified revenue threshold—that provides a quick way both to sanity-check an idea and get insight into its business model:

1. It starts with the desired answer you already determined. For example, a few years ago Innosight was considering creating a new offering: it would provide training material to companies looking to

help middle and junior managers develop innovation skills. We decided that we needed a path to $6 million in revenue to investigate the idea.

2. With the answer in hand, determine the *population* of potential customers. Define it as narrowly as possible—none of this "if we got $1 from every consumer in India" stuff. Innosight assumed that there would be about a thousand companies that cared enough about innovation to invest in widespread training, and that each company would train a thousand managers, making the target population 1 million.

3. Next, assert the *price* of your offering. Innosight assumed it would charge $100 for training materials.

4. Then, assess the *purchase frequency.* Is this a one-time purchase? A consumable good that people purchase a few times a year? Or a rental that essentially is a daily purchase? For our training material, we assumed a company would purchase it every three years, so we put in 0.33.

5. Finally, calculate the required *penetration* to achieve your target. The answer in our case was about 18 percent. That's a pretty high number, which led to immediate questions, such as: Can the price be higher? Are we being too conservative about the market size? Can we charge an up-front fee or

FIGURE 3-1

4P calculation for Innosight's training idea

Steady-state revenue target	$6,000,000	*Ensure the organization has alignment on a steady-state number that would be attractive.*
A. Core population	1,000,000	*Define as tightly as possible what constitutes your "dream customers."*
B. Transaction pricing	$100	*How much will the customer pay per transaction? What data supports this?*
C. Purchase frequency	0.33	*How many purchases are there a year?*
Required penetration	18%	*Solve for this by dividing the revenue target by A × B × C.*

create an ongoing licensing revenue stream? Or is this just not worth it?

That's solid learning from a five-minute exercise! Figure 3-1 summarizes this analysis.

Thinking through the population, price, purchase frequency, and required penetration takes just a few minutes, but it provides rich insight into the viability of your business model.

2. Create a Two-Variable "Spot Sensitivity Table"

This approach zeroes in on two critical variables in the economic model (which could very well be price, penetration, population, or purchase frequency) and looks at how outcomes vary based on changes in each variable. It often serves as a useful way to get a rough view of how big an idea could be and can serve as an early sanity check as to whether achieving financial targets is feasible.

Here's how we used the technique to help an Indian refrigerator manufacturer get more excited about the opportunity to approach its market in a new way. A few years ago, Godrej & Boyce was trying to find a way to compete more effectively against multinational giants such as Samsung, General Electric, and Whirlpool. A quick analysis of the Indian market showed that only about 20 percent of households actually owned a refrigerator. Some of the 80 percent that didn't lacked sufficient wealth to even dream of having a refrigerator, but a sizable portion of the emerging middle class had other constraints. Perhaps they lived in a place that lacked reliable power (it isn't unusual for big cities in India to have up to eight hours a day without power). Or they lived in places that were just too small to house traditional refrigerators. To reach this market, would it make sense to create a lower-priced, smaller product that could be battery-powered?

As the team sought to answer this question, management wondered whether the market opportunity was sufficient to justify investment. We built a simple spot sensitivity table that showed the relationship between household penetration, unit price, and revenues. That calculation raised other uncertainties, most notably the percent of nonconsuming households that could really be targeted and the degree to which target households really had sufficient purchasing power to support desired pricing points.

Those unknowns could be reduced through further study and some focused transaction testing. Godrej ultimately piloted the product under the name ChotuKool in 2009. Successful pilots led to national expansion in 2011, setting the stage for an entire line of products targeting India's emerging middle class.

3. Build a Reverse Income Statement

One of the most practical *Harvard Business Review* articles of the past twenty years is Rita Gunther McGrath and Ian MacMillan's 1995 classic "Discovery-Driven Planning." That article advanced the notion that when assumptions are high and knowledge is low, innovators should follow a different approach to planning. A key component is what McGrath and MacMillan dubbed a *reverse income statement.* Visually, a reverse income statement looks like a decision tree. On the left side of the page is a single box with the answer—the desired profit that a business should produce, or its revenue. The next column splits that answer into no more than three variables. The next column splits each of those boxes into no more than three variables. And so on.

Consider Innosight's training business described above. While the 4P calculation started with a desired revenue target, its reverse income statement starts with a profit target. In this case, imagine we hoped to generate $3 million in profits annually, with margins of at least 50 percent. To the right would be revenues and costs. A target margin of at least 50 percent means the smallest acceptable revenue number would be $6 million, and there would be $3 million in allowable costs. To the right of revenues would be the number of customers and annual revenues per customer. Revenues per customer could be either up-front fees or materials revenue. Materials revenue would be a function of the number of students per company and the materials fee per student. One key cost would be account managers, who could each handle a certain number of companies.

Figure 3-2 shows the reverse income statement for our training business in action. The boxes with dotted fills are assertions or assumptions. By guessing how many students

FIGURE 3-2

Reverse income statement for Innosight's training business

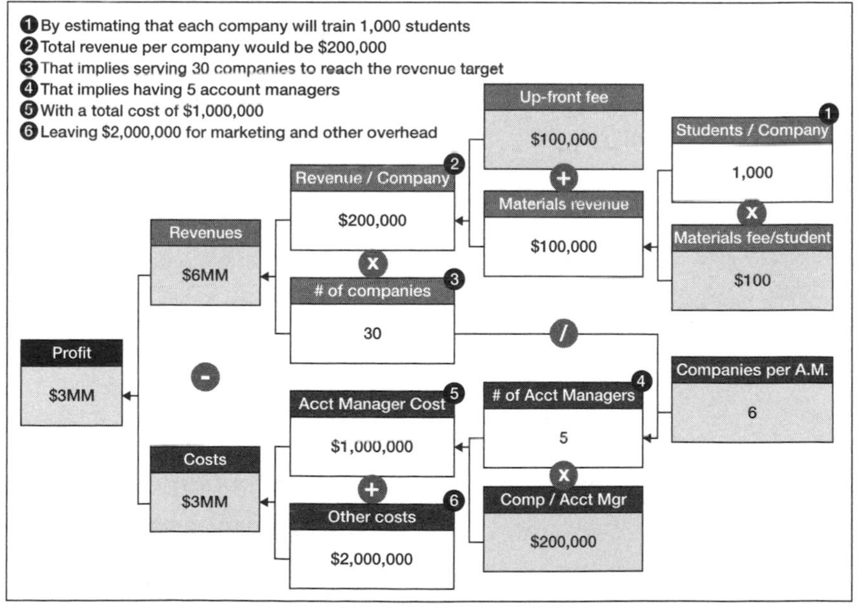

per company we could target (in this case, one thousand), and assuming how many companies each account manager could handle (we guessed six), we could see how many companies we would need to serve, the number of account managers we would need, and how much money would be "left over" for marketing and other activities (in this case, $2 million). There are a lot of assumptions behind the analysis, but seeing the results of simple logic can be very helpful.

Such a tree can get quite complicated, but it provides a very useful way to visualize a business. Filling in some of the boxes on the tree will involve nothing more than educated guesses, but seeing how those guesses flow through to a business can help to highlight uncertainties. Our tree raised questions such as:

- How many people will a company really want to train?
- How much do training companies charge for materials?
- How many people will we need to sell business and service accounts?
- How much room would we have for marketing activities?

4. Construct a Simulation

The business world is complex, making it difficult to model even a seemingly simple business. Businesses can be affected by a range of external factors. There can be complicated feedback loops that can affect a business. Momentum can matter a great deal. Coming up with a single point estimate for a factor such as unit sales in such a complicated world seems wholly inadequate. Fortunately, there are relatively simple tools that can help with financial analysis in the face of this uncertainty. One popular approach is known as Monte Carlo simulation. In essence, a Monte Carlo model runs thousands of simulations, with each simulation randomly modifying each variable according to an inputted distribution. For example, one variable could be *binary*, meaning some percent of the time it is one, some percent of the time it is zero. Another might be evenly distributed among five different outcomes. A third might follow a classic bell curve. Relatively straightforward Microsoft Excel add-ons such as Crystal Ball make the process fairly simple.

We used the technique when advising a team at Procter & Gamble about ten years ago. The team was working on a novel probiotic solution that promised to restore digestive balance to consumers who suffered from conditions like irritable bowel syndrome. The team seemed to have all the ingredients of a successful business. They had a proprietary solution, licensed from a university in Ireland. They were targeting a pressing consumer problem that lacked good solutions. To be effective, the product had to be taken every day, creating a financially attractive business model. However, initial market research by a third party suggested that demand was too low to justify future investment. Our goal was to identify the most critical financial assumptions to make the case to management that a relatively modest investment could prove that the market research was wrong.

Our financial model had only five variables:

- The total addressable population
- The percentage of that population who would try the product once ("trial")
- The percentage of people who tried the product once who would repeat ("repeat")
- The number of repeat purchases per repeater ("repeats per repeater")
- The price per transaction

While we were pretty certain about the total addressable population and had a good sense as to what pricing would look like, trial, repeat, and repeats per repeater were nothing more than good guesses. Fortunately, through P&G's rich databases, we could at least get some bounds for each variable and make reasonable guesses around the potential distribution and relationship between them (for example, the higher the ratio of repeat to trial, the more likely repeats per repeater would be higher as it indicated a scenario where the product really "clicked" with the consumer). Figure 3-3 shows the results of a preliminary run of the model.

The effort produced two pieces of insight. First, while there were plenty of scenarios in which the product was

FIGURE 3-3

Preliminary run of Monte Carlo model for P&G's probiotic idea

Forecast: B5 **Cell: B5**

Summary:

Display Range is from $1,596,467 to $435,702,128
Entire Range is from $1,050,841 to $688,755,205
After 10,000 Trials, the Std. Error of the Mean is $856,875

Statistics:	**Value**
Trials	10,000
Mean	$216,849,383
Median	$212,411,506
Mode	---
Standard Deviation	$85,687,527
Variance	7E+15
Skewness	0.34
Kurtosis	3.21
Coeff. of Variability	0.40
Range Minimum	$1,050,841
Range Maximum	$688,755,205
Range Width	$687,704,364
Mean Std. Error	$856,875.27

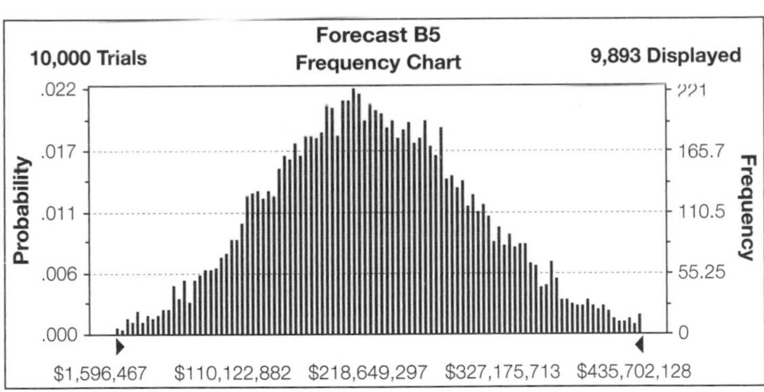

a dud, there were also plenty where it was a big hit. The large size of the market, the potential for high repeat purchase, and a reasonable price point created circumstances where the upside could be quite large. Second, repeats per repeater really was the variable on which success hinged. If that number were high enough, even relatively small penetration numbers would support an adequately sized business. The team used the data to get management to invest in a small-scale in-market trial to figure out how frequently people who actually experienced the product would purchase it again. Positive results ultimately led to an increase in investment, and full national launch of the product—under the brand name Align—in the United States in 2010.

Role-Playing

A third lens to use to evaluate an idea is a simple but powerful one. It involves listing out all of the major stakeholders in an idea and role-playing how they experience the idea. Consider acting out a sales pitch to a customer, a conversation with a supplier, or even how you would convince recalcitrant management to invest in the idea. One of the general truths that innovators often overlook is that people don't do what doesn't make sense to them.[1] Looking at an idea from other perspectives can help to unearth weak links in an idea early.

1. Sorry for the intentional double negative.

The other advantage of this technique is it can help you sharpen your ability to sell an idea. Make no mistake: every innovator is at her heart a great salesperson. *The Little Black Book of Innovation* noted how innovators need to:

- Convince customers to buy something they have never bought before
- Get skeptical senior management to invest in doing something different
- Pry money out of the hands of tightfisted venture capitalists
- Urge friends or coworkers to join an underfunded business that statistics suggest is going to fail
- Cajole a reticent department to free up a resource
- Push a team to continue forward when bad news inevitably strikes

If you are stuck, start by walking through a single transaction, when the customer consumes a product or service and money is exchanged. Transactions can be simple: a plumber comes to my house, spends an hour fixing a leaky faucet, and I pay him an hourly rate in cash. Or they can be complicated, sometimes maddeningly so. Consider filing an insurance claim, or seeking reimbursement for a medical procedure. In both examples, complicated chains of interrelated activities come together to make the transaction happen. If any piece of a chain breaks, then the transaction never happens.

Key Messages from This Chapter

1. Evaluate an idea from multiple perspectives to get a sense as to its strengths, weaknesses, and uncertainties.
2. Use financial modeling techniques, but remember that an awesome spreadsheet and an awesome business are two distinctly different things.
3. Remember that the goal is not to make a decision but to figure out what unknowns might need to be addressed.

CHAPTER 4

Focus

While the end result of innovation can be breathtakingly simple, the process is anything but. Getting dozens of things to work together can overwhelm even the most experienced innovator. The key to speeding through the first mile is to focus on *strategic uncertainties* that have the most potential to derail the business—or to serve as the backbone of a sustainable strategy. This chapter provides more information on different types of strategic uncertainties, and then describes how to prioritize the most critical ones.

First, a definition. Dictionary.com says that something that is *uncertain* is "Not able to be relied on; not known or definite." Uncertainties contrast to *facts*, which Dictionary.com defines as "Something that actually exists; reality; truth."

These are clearly different things—facts have happened; uncertainties are what could happen—but the two are often confused. As a simple exercise, look at the following five sentences and quickly assess whether each is a fact:

1. Our revenues grew 12 percent last year.
2. My wife will be happy if I bring home nice flowers.

3. The population of China is 1.351 billion.

4. If we raise prices, our volumes will decrease.

5. Demand for our product will be low, as few consumers said they would buy it when we asked them.

The first sentence looks like a pretty solid fact—but it assumes your accounting department did its job or that there won't be some future event that causes you to re-evaluate past revenue. The second one is an assumption (though experimentation has validated that it is true most of the time). The third is a fact. Or is it? That depends on whether you trust government statistics. Executives typically state the fourth item as a fact, but sometimes it is true and sometimes it is not. The fifth feels like a fact because we've researched it, but the reality (as discussed below) is that what people *say* they will do and what they *actually* do are frequently two different things.

The reality is, the world of business contains fewer hard facts than we would like. One of the simplest indicators that you are uncertain about something is when you start a sentence with "I think." Almost by definition, any new idea is rife with strategic uncertainty. When you are doing something that hasn't quite been done before, there will be many uncertainties.

Documenting and evaluating an idea are vital components of teasing out uncertainties. If you haven't already created a list of key uncertainties behind your idea, go back to the work you did in conjunction with chapters 2 and 3 and do so now. Go for breadth—don't stop until you have at least fifty uncertainties on your list.

A raw list of more than fifty items can be hard to process, so consider creating a visual depiction of uncertainties to identify areas that have the most impact on the overall business. Simple mind-mapping tools can be good ways to visualize the relationships between uncertainties. They help in the next critical phase of the process: picking out the most critical strategic uncertainties.

How to Prioritize Uncertainties

Our 2008 book, *The Innovator's Guide to Growth*, featured a simple 2-by-2 chart to help to tease out the most important uncertainties to address. It essentially involves asking two questions:

1. How confident are you in a given area?
2. How much impact would it have if you are wrong?

Let's address each question.

Assessing Confidence

Academic studies consistently find that most humans aren't particularly good at understanding risk and probabilities (see appendix B for more on the biases that make the first mile so tough). We consistently:

- Overstate our ability to control events that are largely dictated by chance
- Overstate our confidence in assessing outcomes that have wide ranges
- Underestimate risks
- Ignore *black swan* events—rare but high-impact occurrences

One general theme of the DEFT process is being as humble as possible about what truly is a fact and what is an uncertainty (or, occasionally, a wish). Generally speaking, the further you go from your core business, the less you know and the more you assume. While people generally agree with that statement, human biases mean they underestimate how much less they know and how much more they assume. Figure 4-1 displays this graphically. While people assume knowledge goes down, they assume a shallower trajectory than reality. The result? A deadly combination of false confidence in some areas and missed assumptions in others.

The Innovator's Guide to Growth had a simple litmus test to assess confidence in an assertion: How much of your salary would you be willing to put on the line? Would you be willing to risk a year's salary? A month's salary? A week's salary? Or just a day's salary? This framing often quickly gets people to realize that they are not quite as confident as they first thought.

Another way to develop a better grounding of true levels of confidence in an idea is to use table 4-1. It looks at

FIGURE 4-1

The further you go, the less you know

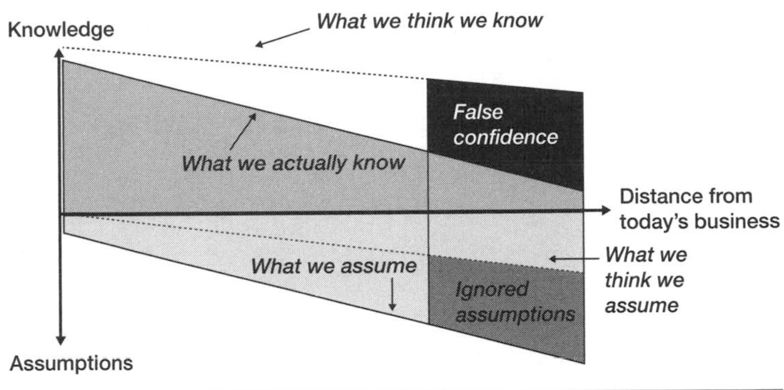

the three key questions introduced in chapter 2 (Is there a need? Can you deliver? Is it worth it?) and provides a quick way to gauge confidence in each area. The further to the left side of the table for each area, the greater the uncertainty. The text that follows provides an explanation for each cell in the table.

IS THERE A NEED?

- Said: If a customer has said she wants something, you know next to nothing about whether or not she *really* wants something, let alone whether she will pay for it. Put in more blunt terms, people lie. Not because they are bad people, but because they just aren't good at projecting future behavior. Many people can't even remember what they had for breakfast; what they say they will do in the

TABLE 4-1

First mile certainty table

Question	Low →		Degree of certainty		→ High	
Is there a need?	Said	Shown	Used	Purchased	Repeated	Advocated
Can you deliver?	Dreamed	Drawn	Prototyped	Piloted	Delivered	Scaled
Is it worth it?	Envelope model	Transaction model	Business plan	Unit economics validated	Line of sight to profitability	Sustainable profitable business

future in many cases is nothing more than a wild guess.

- **Shown:** A more reliable gauge of a customer need is when someone is already spending money or time to solve a problem. That is a signal that the problem is in fact important to him.

- **Used:** Confidence goes up when a customer gets a chance to actually use a new product or service. A need she couldn't articulate suddenly becomes clear once she holds the thing in her hand, experiences the benefit, and continues to use it.

- **Purchased:** As the old saying goes, "Money talks." A tipping point in confidence comes when a customer agrees to part with his hard-earned cash or chooses to spend time with a particular solution.

- **Repeated:** Of course, for many ideas a single purchase is not enough to make a business, or else the makers of Pet Rocks and bread makers would be phenomenal success stories. When a customer repeatedly purchases or uses something, it signals that you have hit on a deep need.

- **Advocated:** As Fred Reichheld demonstrated in his *Harvard Business Review* classic "The One Number You Need to Grow," one of the strongest litmus tests of customer loyalty is the answer to the simple question, "How likely is it that you would recommend this to a friend or colleague?" The passion that breeds advocacy is a powerful signal of an idea that addresses a very deep need.

CAN YOU DELIVER?

- **Dreamed:** Almost every idea starts in relatively rough form. There's nothing wrong with that—as long as you don't confuse a dream with reality. You have to find ways to make your dream tangible.
- **Drawn:** A good way to begin to get a sense of an idea's feasibility is to simply draw it on a piece of paper. If it is a service, map out the way the customer will experience it. This simple activity can often highlight previously hidden things that need to go right in order for success.
- **Prototyped:** A functional prototype provides a step change in confidence that delivery is possible. Prototypes are not just for physical products: you

can (and should) prototype a service or even a business model.

- **Piloted:** Of course, it's easy enough to do something once in controlled conditions. But what about when you actually get into the marketplace? That's when the famous Rumsfeldian "unknown unknowns" begin to appear. A pilot, or controlled market test, further increases confidence in an idea's feasibility.
- **Delivered:** The next step beyond a pilot is to begin to commercialize an idea. Once you have delivered in "normal" conditions, you begin to get a better sense as to competitive response and long-term issues that are easy to ignore in a pilot.
- **Scaled:** Early-stage success is great, but you can only truly be confident in an idea's sustainability when you have scaled it to more customers in more markets.

IS IT WORTH IT?

- **Envelope model:** Calculating an idea's potential often starts on a cocktail napkin or the back of an envelope. The small space forces simple mathematical equations, which can actually be very helpful means to learn about an idea (the 4P calculation described in chapter 3 is an example of an envelope model) but obviously shouldn't be the basis of big investments.

- Transaction model: The next move from a cocktail napkin is working out the economics of an individual transaction. How much will a customer pay? What will it cost to create the thing that the customer will purchase? Who else gets a cut? Walking through a single transaction begins to bring the economics into clarity.

- Business model: Most corporate innovators and many entrepreneurs are familiar with detailed business models, spreadsheets that detail how an idea generates profits and free cash flow. Note that a business model will likely leave you with still relatively low levels of confidence that an idea is worth it. After all, a business model simply reports a series of mathematical relationships. So it is important to go beyond spreadsheets to seeing what the business looks like in action.

- Unit economics validated: The first moment of truth for economic viability is when an innovator develops robust understanding of how an *actual* transaction with real people and real money works. When you can sell something for more than it costs to deliver it, or you have a market-grounded plan for how to get costs low enough (or price high enough) to cross this milestone, you are on your way to success.

- Line of sight to profitability: One of the most common debates innovators have is whether it is better to get big fast and grab customers or try to build a profitable business. Once every five years, a company executes a land-grab strategy and succeeds. Hundreds more execute the same strategy and fail. A line of sight to profitability means that an innovator could choose to have a profitable business, or it could choose to make investments to drive growth. When that's a choice rather than a necessity, it means you are getting close to breaking through.

- Sustainable profitable business: Clearly, once a business provides cash flows, it has passed the "Is it worth it?" test![1]

While the above items are all framed in the context of a commercial idea, it is easy enough to reframe any of them for an idea to improve a process or cut costs. Rough models and early mock-ups provide directional confidence, sophisticated models and early market data sharpen that confidence, but demonstrated impact is required before you can be confident that the idea will truly create value.

The simplicity of the first mile certainty table makes it a great tool for team discussion. Print out the template from our companion website and gain consensus as to today's level of knowledge. Select an experiment from the "experiment cookbook" described in chapter 6 that will move you

1. As my favorite reviewer Lib Gibson noted, "A bit simplistic. I always think a good CEO's job is to ditch good ideas in order to free resources to go after great ideas. So just being profitable doesn't make it slam-dunk true that it's worth it." A subtle point, but a good one.

to the right in an area where your knowledge is low. Revisit the chart on a quarterly basis.

Assessing Impact

All things being equal, you should focus on uncertainties that have the biggest impact on your idea's viability. A 2010 *Harvard Business Review* article by former Innosight managing partner Matt Eyring and Innosight adviser Clark Gilbert (currently the CEO of Deseret News and Deseret Digital) highlights two particular types of uncertainties that should rise to the top of anyone's list.

The first is what Gilbert and Eyring call a *deal killer*. This is an uncertainty that risks the entire venture. For example, a deal killer for a medical device company would be getting approval from regulatory bodies. Many deal killers are discrete probabilities—there is a certain percentage chance that they will occur. Make sure you understand what tools are at your disposal to shift odds in your favor. For example, when a company submits a new drug to the US Food and Drug Administration, historical statistics suggest that some percentage will get approved and some won't. Further, the amount of time it will take varies. A company naturally should study these past events to understand the real chances of success and understand what can influence the outcome. Also be on the lookout for black swan events that might be low probability but would have disastrous consequences.

The other critical category of uncertainty is what Gilbert and Eyring call a *path dependency*, which is an uncertainty that affects subsequent strategic choices. If you have created a mind map or system dynamics visual of your uncertainties, path dependencies tend to be areas on the chart that have lots of connections to other elements. The choice of the target customer is often a critical path dependency—the channel to market, pricing model, marketing approach, and so on depend vitally on that target customer. Path dependencies are areas that should be addressed early.

As an example, in 2012, Innosight explored the possibility of creating a new business focused on building products that could be used in conjunction with its advisory services. What if, for example, clients could download a tool to help them build reverse income statements and prioritize assumptions, assess an uncertain strategy, or even assess their own capabilities as an innovator? There were dozens of uncertainties, but several that appeared to be deal killers or path dependencies:

- **Deal killer:** We can create a compelling product for less than $250,000.
- **Deal killer:** There is market demand for supportive products.
- **Path dependency:** We should start with an assessment product targeted at individuals seeking to become better innovators.

As much as we could, we focused on addressing those three areas as we moved our idea from the planning phase to the testing phase.

FIGURE 4-2

How to prioritize uncertainties

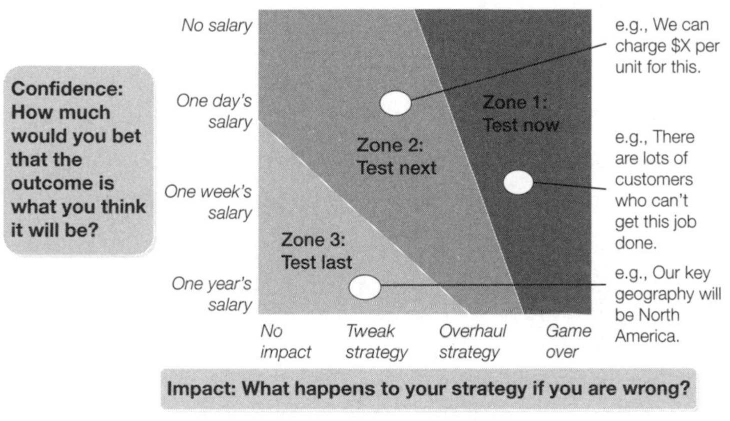

To bring the elements discussed in this section together, map the most critical uncertainties on a 2-by-2 chart like the one pictured in figure 4-2, with impact (low to high) on one axis and certainty (high to low) on the other. Pay particular attention to the upper-right quadrant, where certainty is low and impact is high. Don't worry too much about the lower-left quadrant. Consider a third filter—what is the complexity of learning more? Seek to test areas that you can address quickly and cheaply. That might mean addressing a less critical uncertainty if you can knock it off easily. You might, with a degree of trepidation, leave the most critical unknown for later if addressing it looks too onerous and there are other potential uncertainties that could derail or influence the business.

If you are more quantitatively oriented, build a simple spreadsheet that assigns a number value to each area (low numbers for low impact, high certainty, and expensive tests; higher numbers for greater impact, less uncertainty, and cheaper tests). Multiply the impact and certainty numbers, add the test complexity number, and focus on the highest numbers (the companion website has a simple spreadsheet to help with this). Never be a slave to the numbers—if instinct tells you something that scores low actually is critically important, add it to your list of focus uncertainties.

Keys to Success

The focus stage of the DEFT process is critical because it serves as a way to synthesize the previous two stages and determines what you do in the final stage. It is also a stage where it is easy to make mistakes. To maximize productivity in this stage, remember three critical success factors:

1. Focus on the few. When everything is important, nothing is important. The end result of the focus stage should be a list of no more than six specific uncertainties. And, ideally, that list really boils down to one or two critical questions. There's nothing wrong with having a longer watch list that you monitor on a regular basis to see if things change, but if you don't focus efforts, it is too easy to get drowned in complexity.

2. **Do your homework.** Remember, most human beings overstate confidence in uncertain areas. Keep your eye out for data that builds confidence that something that you think is a fact is in fact a fact. Consider specifically some of the "if you have an hour" experiments described in chapter 6, such as conducting web research into comparable efforts or talking to subject-matter experts.

3. **Involve outsiders.** Our brains can be our biggest enemies when it comes to making realistic assessments of certainty. One time-tested way to fight back against this limitation is to ensure that noninvolved outsiders participate in the process. While outsiders might not have expertise in all of the elements of your idea, they can offer grounded perspectives that help to keep the process honest. In fact, that lack of expertise might help them to find a creative solution that you hadn't yet considered. Look specifically for people who have intuition around innovation, such as experienced entrepreneurs or venture capitalists.

Key Messages from This Chapter

1. We aren't great at accurately assessing uncertainty—be humble when you assess how much you really know.

2. Use the first mile certainty table to get a grounded view of how confident you should be about the robustness of your idea.
3. Not all uncertainties are the same—pay particular attention to deal killers and path dependencies.

CHAPTER 5

Test, Learn, and Adjust

The final part of the DEFT process is the most important—the design and execution of tests, or experiments, to address the most critical uncertainties. Experiment design and management might feel unfamiliar to many businesspeople. However, for centuries scientists have honed a particular approach to managing uncertainty. At its heart, the so-called scientific method is simple. It starts with a question you want to investigate. You then form a hypothesis and make a prediction related to the hypothesis. You then design an experiment to test the prediction. You ensure that you have a way to measure the experiment. You conduct the experiment and analyze the results. The method involves a healthy skepticism, with a high burden of proof required to reject the so-called null hypothesis that the hypothesis is in fact false, and demands for repeatability before an experiment's results are accepted.

While every experiment has its own nuances, the text below details six keys to successfully designing and executing experiments. The first four cover experiment design and team formation, and the last two detail how to extract learning and make appropriate decisions. The chapter ends with a case study showing these principles in action; chapter 6 provides more granular guidance around more than a dozen specific experiments.

1. Keep Teams Small and Focused

Everyone knows that small teams generally move faster than large teams, yet big companies frequently drown growth initiatives by staffing them with functions that mirror the core business. It's tempting to do so, because in big companies flooding a team with resources signals the team's importance publicly, attracting stars that connect their importance to the range of resources they control or influence. But complexity quickly sets in. The legal representative, for example, identifies a number of critical regulatory and intellectual property–related areas. The marketer who has run thousands of focus groups starts organizing focus groups around the country. The regulatory representative starts dealing with a plan to get approval in all fifty US states. Working on many simultaneous issues dramatically slows progress.[1]

1. There's a wonderful academic term for this problem: *Penrosian Slack*. The name comes from an arcane 1950s book by Edith Penrose called *The Theory of the Growth of the Firm*. Unless you are academically inclined, avoid the book—Penrose had a particularly dense, inaccessible writing style. But there is a cen-

For example, one team I advised had thirteen members, including representatives from the legal department, marketing, and product supply. The team manager gamely had to knit together a complicated plan to get regulatory approval in multiple countries, a detailed launch plan, and assessment of multiple suppliers. Project meetings would go on for hours as representatives from each function reported on their progress and the team debated endless scenarios. Keep in mind—this was before it was clear that the product they were working on was technologically feasible, and, even if it was, if there was any consumer interest. It was no surprise that senior management complained about the team's slow pace. The legal, marketing, and product supply representatives were doing their jobs, but the unnecessary effort dramatically slowed the project team.

Contrast that thirteen-person team to most start-up companies, where a very small team swarms the most critical problem facing the business. The team figures out "good enough" solutions to other, less critical problems or defers them until later in the process. After all, there's no point in solving multicountry regulatory issues if you can't

---

tral tenet that helped to spur what is now known as the *resource-based* view of the firm, which in essence holds that strategy doesn't drive resource allocation; the way in which resources are allocated determines strategy. Penrose argued that you could tell a company's future strategy by looking at its slack capacity, because the slack capacity always gets filled. So an idle manufacturing line starts running, a salesperson with time on her hands starts making sales calls, and so on. Filling the slack capacity pulls the company's strategy in a certain direction.

demonstrate basic demand for a product. For example, for many years I moonlighted as Innosight's chief financial officer. I didn't have the specialized skills required for the role in a large organization, but I was adequate (with the support of key team members) in our business's early days.

Small teams have their downsides. By definition, a small team can't have the range of capabilities that a large team has. That means biasing for people whose skills look like a "T." That is, they have deep skills in a particular area but also have a wide range of skills that can help with a range of problems. Looking for "T"s? Ask a small group of people to highlight skills they have that their colleagues might not know about. It's surprising how even people who have worked together for years can lack this kind of understanding!

If necessity is indeed the mother of invention, scarcity is its midwife. Jeff Bezos from Amazon.com suggests a "two pizza" rule for team size—keep a team small enough that it can be fed with two pizzas. If it needs more than two, cut the team size so it can move faster.

Lean and mean teams speed through innovation's first mile by focusing on the most critical uncertainties. It seems natural to want to learn as much as possible whenever you run an experiment. So if you test a concept with consumers, you might seek to understand price sensitivity, marketing effectiveness, supply chain dynamics, postsales service strategies, package design, and more. The problem is, the more things you try to learn at once, the more difficult it is to determine what you really learned. Focusing on one or two critical areas seems limiting, but it helps to capture the most important learning.

Don't test things that you already know. For example, one thing that sometimes makes companies hesitant to innovate is the risk that a cherished brand will be compromised if it is attached to a new offering. But why does a test need to be branded? Customers might react to the brand instead of the product, providing a false signal of interest. Companies already have a pretty good sense of the power of their brand. Consider running tests with no brands at all. If something succeeds without a brand, imagine how much better it will do when powered by a trusted brand!

Focus also means not being obsessed about statistical significance. Of course, if you can reach a statistically meaningful population, do so. But prioritize speed and affordability, even if it means the sample size is "just good enough."

Another way to reinforce focus is to set tight time frames. Ninety days is an effective number. It might appear impossible to develop a prototype or earn revenues in that time frame, but scarcity often forces creative approaches that lead to rapid, high-impact learning.

2. Design Tests Carefully

Steven Spear's wonderful book *The High-Velocity Edge* contains a detailed case study of the US nuclear submarine program. The first nuclear submarine (the *Nautilus*) was launched in 1954, a mere five years after the start of the nuclear propulsion program. Despite a ridiculously complex set of technologies, in six decades, the US program has not suffered a single serious incident related to the nuclear reactor. Contrast that to the Russian program, which has suffered a series of incidents costing at least twenty-seven lives, scuttling several submarines, and releasing radioactive material into the atmosphere.[2]

Spear explained that at least one reason for the United States' success is the disciplined way in which it approached learning. The program's founder, Hyman Rickover, believed in the "discipline of engineering." Nothing would be done randomly. Engineers had to come up with a hypothesis before they designed a new component or system. They had to make explicit their very best understanding and expectation of what actions would lead to what outcomes. They then had to design systems that would allow them to measure how well their hypothesis held up. "With expectations clear, it would be obvious when something happened that didn't conform to those expectations," Spear wrote. "As a result, even if you didn't succeed, you created an opportunity to learn to succeed. Stating clear expectations was a given, with no exceptions."

One vivid example of this principle at work was the design of radiation shielding for the ships' nuclear reactors. As Spear writes:

2. The title of the relevant table from Spear's book says it all: "Partial List of Calamities in the Soviet Nuclear Navy."

> No one knew how neutron bombardment would fatigue the metal and how the piping's welds, joints and bends would affect radiation patterns. Therefore, when it was time to test the shielding, a grid was laid over the surface, with sensors distributed all across it. But the evaluation didn't rest at that. Before any measurements were taken, Rockwell [Theodore Rockwell, Rickover's technical director] insisted that predictions be made about what the measurements at each point would be. It was not sufficient to find out if the various sections passed or failed in terms of emitted radiation. Rockwell and his colleagues already knew that they would be wrong at many points since the science and technology were still in early stages. Therefore, they wanted to know for certain—sooner rather than later—exactly where and when they were wrong and what they misunderstood. The sensors were not just there to make safe and unsafe situations. They were there to identify pockets of ignorance on the part of the shielding designers. That is why, rather than just recording readings and noting where the exposure was too high, they first predicted what the readings would be and then compared those predictions to the actual readings to discover where their understanding was confirmed and where it was refuted.

To make this principle real, make sure any experiment has a chart like the one that appears in figure 5-1. It starts

FIGURE 5-1

HOPE experimentation template

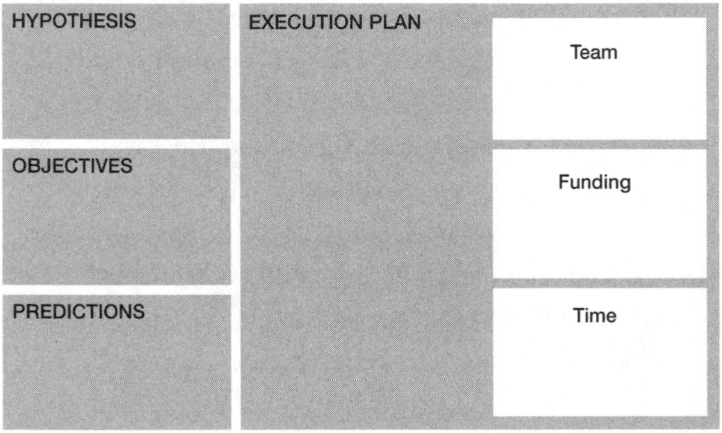

HYPOTHESIS	EXECUTION PLAN	Team
OBJECTIVES		Funding
PREDICTIONS		Time

with the *hypothesis* you plan to test. Then come test *objectives*. Why does testing this hypothesis matter? Next are the specific *predictions* about what the test will show, which forces you to think about how you will measure results. It will be hard to make specific predictions for areas in which you are just speculating, but the discipline will help you begin to determine cause and effect, and wire you to extract the right learning from your efforts. Finally, detail how you will *execute* the experiments, including the team and funding you require and how long it will take. Remember the acronym HOPE: hypothesis, objectives, prediction, and execution.

Careful experiment design helps to determine the optimal team makeup by pinpointing required expertise. For example, if you plan to sell a small quantity of products over the web, ideally someone on the team knows something about e-commerce. Be careful about including any expert whose skills lie in areas that are not on the experiment plan; if you do, be prepared for progress to slow.

3. Aim to Learn in the Market

To make steel strong, you have to forget it at temperatures above 2000°F. To make a business idea strong, you should forge it in the white-hot heat of the marketplace. Yet, too frequently, strategies are forged in the languid glow of conference room lights. Typical activities include analyzing market research reports, creating complicated Excel spreadsheets, and developing thick PowerPoint decks. The documents that result from this effort are mighty, but the insights are surprisingly brittle, failing to hold up to scrutiny.

Financial forecasts are often a telltale sign of where a team has done its learning. Forecasts with precise point estimates that carry two numbers to the right of the decimal point often result from a team leaning heavily on analysts' detailed market projections. Certainly, market-intelligence companies like IDC, Nielsen, and Gartner produce high-quality work. But estimates of the size and growth characteristics of new markets are notoriously inaccurate. Team members should instead be spending time in the field talking to potential customers, ideally armed with a prototype or mock-up. Negative reactions aren't necessary bad, by the way, as long as the team draws learnings and modifies its approach appropriately.

One way to ensure there is an appropriate bias to action is to track the ratio of the time spent preparing for and attending internal meetings to time spent in the market. Any ratio higher than 1:3 should raise eyebrows.

4. Maximize Flexibility

The more complicated the test, the more likely that something completely unanticipated will happen somewhere along the way. In some cases, that learning might lead to minor modifications. In some cases, like when a new unknown surfaces or a deal killer can't be adequately overcome, there might be a need for a major overhaul. As you begin executing your test, create as much flexibility as possible to create room for course correction. Consider the following rules of thumb:

- Prototype before you build.
- Fake it before you make it.[3]
- Borrow before you buy.
- Contract before you hire.

3. The idea here goes beyond vaporware. Consider a fake course in a university course catalog to gauge student interest or a website that doesn't have functionality to sense market demand.

- Test before you commit.
- Research before you do it.
- Outsource before you ramp up.

The general rule is to keep fixed costs as low as possible, as fixed costs can make it hard to make the micro course corrections that so often presage success. Flexibility isn't free, so there might be some muttering about money wasting, but in the long run the flexibility is well worth it.

Flexibility often requires tapping into external resources. Too frequently, teams inside companies assume that the only resources at their disposal are those that exist in their department or building. It's as though someone has placed a dome over them, setting clear boundaries on their innovation ecosystem. They then complain that they can't make progress because they can't access resources that are tied up in activities that support the core business. Remember Harvard's Howard Stevenson's definition of entrepreneurship—the pursuit of opportunity without regard to resources currently controlled—to break the dome. Teams running tests should look beyond the corporate dome to tap into the ample and awesome free or low-cost resources available to entrepreneurs. The first form of financing for most start-ups is their credit card, so a lack of financial resources simply isn't an acceptable excuse for a lack of progress. Consider using the following free or low-cost tools to help with key issues:

- Designing marketing materials or other collateral: Elance.com

- Performing repetitive tasks that can't be completely automated: Amazon Mechanical Turk
- Creating a mock-up: Google Sketch
- Project management: Basecamp
- Finding experts: LinkedIn
- Market research: SurveyMonkey.com
- Website design: Wix.com
- Branding and logos: 99designs.com
- File sharing: Dropbox.com

These solutions might feel a bit frightening to people inside large corporations who are used to using more robust solutions, but they are affordable and extremely effective.

One way to ensure flexibility is to carefully stage investment in a new idea. Venture capitalists do this intuitively. They give a company a slug of money to address a critical uncertainty. If the company addresses it, it gets a follow-up dose to knock off the next one. Generally, there are five questions in the life of an idea:

1. **Should I build a plan?** At this stage, you have the spark of an idea and should conduct basic research to figure out whether it is worth investing the time to flesh out the idea in more detail.
2. **Should I run a low-cost test?** Quick-hit research hasn't highlighted any laws-of-physics deal killers, so it is

time to do more extensive homework to determine whether it is worth investing in more market-facing experiments.

3. **Should I run a pilot?** Assuming the low-cost tests look promising, the next step is to contemplate whether to run a more comprehensive test.
4. **Should we launch?** This question asks whether the results of the pilot suggest launching the business (most likely after some modifications).
5. **Should we scale?** Search mode has ended. If the deal-killing risks are addressed and the path to profitability is clear, it is now time to step on the gas.

The less you know, the less you ought to invest to ensure you have sufficient flexibility for the course corrections that characterize the first mile.

5. Savor Surprises

The previous four tips help you design effective experiments. You aren't done yet. The next two pointers help to make sure you extract the right learning and take the right action based on that learning.

It is natural to look at the measures you select for your experiments to essentially be go/no-go variables. That is, if you hit or exceed your measure, you ought to proceed. If you don't, you should either course-correct or scupper the effort.

Remember, the goal of an experiment isn't to confirm; it is to learn. Therefore, the operative question in all cases is *why* you exceeded or fell short of a measure. The anomalies—the things you didn't expect—often contain the most interesting findings. There are countless stories of scientific and business breakthroughs that were essentially accidents.

There are two ways to help ensure that you appropriately "savor" these surprises. The first is to have outsiders review the results of the experiments. Without the biases that come from participating in the experiment, the outsiders can often see things that are hidden to the experimenters. The second is to ensure that decision makers have some degree of direct involvement in the experiment. Consider the research of Richard Wiseman of the University of Hertfordshire. Among other things, Wiseman studies luck. He has run a number of research projects to determine whether people can in fact "make their own luck." In one experiment, Wiseman asked groups of people who considered themselves lucky and unlucky to count the number of photographs in a newspaper. It took the unlucky group two minutes to complete the task. The lucky group completed it in *seconds*—because the second page of the newspaper contained a huge message that told the reader that there were forty-three images in the newspaper. Wiseman experimented with putting a large notice in the middle of the newspaper that said "Stop counting. Tell the experimenter you have seen this and win £250." The purported "unlucky" people were so focused on the task at hand that they missed the chance for free money.

The insight from Wiseman's work is critical if you are trying to learn about new opportunities or test ideas. If you completely delegate learning to a third party, that party will dutifully count the pictures in the newspaper and give you a nice glossy report that answers your question, but misses the point. Personal involvement with an eye for the unexpected helps to highlight important anomalies.

6. Take Action Based on the Learning

It is far too easy to treat an experiment as a tick-the-box exercise where you dutifully carry it out, get the results, and then continue with the plan you had before you ran the experiment. Research consistently shows that an innovator's *first* plan and the *right* plan are very different things. As such, it is important to carefully consider what the learning suggests at predetermined milestones. Generally speaking, you can make one of four decisions:

- Accelerate: What you've learned has increased confidence in key assumptions, shown that the impact of potential risks is minimal, or decreased the probability of bad events. It's time to step on the gas.
- Carefully continue: You aren't yet confident enough to throw major resources at your idea, but what you have seen suggests you are still going in the right direction. You might make some minor modifications and proceed with another round of testing.

- Pivot: The term *pivot* entered the lexicon with the 2011 publication of Eric Ries's best-seller *The Lean Startup*. In the book, Ries blended principles of lean manufacturing, the research of Steve Blank, and his start-up experience to provide an entertaining and helpful guide for approaching start-ups in a more scientific way. Countless successful businesses have undergone significant pivots, or strategic course corrections. The strategy that allowed peer-to-peer payment giant PayPal to dominate its space was the so-called Option J—after A, B, C, D, and so forth didn't pan out. Ries's work provides a helpful guide to think about different types of pivots.
- Shut down: Not every idea is destined for greatness; not every start-up is destined to survive. At any juncture, it is always worth asking whether to keep proceeding or whether there is an alternative business idea that warrants deeper attention. If you have followed the guidance of this book, these decisions should be relatively dispassionate, though they are always difficult.

These decisions are rarely crystal clear. Management teams, particularly in large organizations, feel overwhelming pressure to default to the second option and to continue to probe and investigate. One simple trick to avoid this is to make continued exploration the last option rather than the default one. Also consider how the US Marine Corps trains young soldiers to make decisions in the so-called fog of war. The Corps' "70 percent solution" essentially holds that it is better to execute on an imperfect plan than to consider every angle and miss opportunities. Chapter 8 provides further guidance about decision making and disengagement systems that support the DEFT process.

Experiment Design in Action at AsiaCom

A few years ago, an Asian telecommunications company (disguised here as AsiaCom) had an idea for an exciting service, which would essentially turn your phone into a sophisticated tracking device that learned who you were, where you went, and what you liked. Since you always have your phone with you, AsiaCom thought that it had a unique opportunity to couple its ability to obtain information (managing inevitable privacy concerns, of course) with sophisticated data-processing capabilities. This "location-derived insight" could set the stage for such services as real-time deals customized to an individual's location and preferences, selling aggregated information about consumer shopping behavior to retailers, or even insurance packages that were tailored to people's habits.

We guided AsiaCom through the DEFT process. While the idea had the potential to generate multiple revenue streams, we decided to focus on targeted advertising revenue and, more specifically, on three critical hypotheses:

1. AsiaCom could generate unique location-derived insight.

2. Consumers would respond to advertisements based on that insight.

3. Privacy concerns could be managed.

There was strong supporting evidence behind each assumption. Significant investment by venture capitalists in the space suggested ample opportunity. But there was a high degree of uncertainty as well. So the test the company decided to execute was a focused prototype of the hypothesized business model. That meant:

- Designing an application that would sit on the consumers' phone to track location and serve specific deals—without killing the battery
- Creating a data model to capture location information and map that information to specific "points of interest," such as restaurants, health clubs, or shopping malls
- Processing reams of data
- Handling redemption of deals
- Developing mechanisms to handle privacy concerns
- Attracting and managing end users

AsiaCom consciously controlled the number of participants in its pilot to fewer than five hundred to keep operations manageable, but of course it was watching carefully to figure out what it would need to do to successfully scale the business to tens of millions of customers. Consistent with best practices, the team carefully predicted every aspect of the test, even if the predictions were based only on educated guesses.

The prototype ended up taking approximately a year. During the alpha phase, the team worked with a third-party designer to develop a very rough application and used social networks to get thirty customers to download the application. The alpha test helped AsiaCom executives understand operational challenges in more depth and increased the chances that the more complete deployment would deliver against objectives.

In the next phase, the team developed and deployed a more robust application, increased the number of consumers, and began giving specific offers to consumers. We sought simplicity and flexibility wherever we could. For example, we didn't have any "real" advertisers involved, since we didn't need to learn whether advertisers wanted to attract paying customers (they do!). Instead of integrating with merchants to develop complicated redemption systems, the team provided cash to consumers who sent a receipt showing a purchase related to a qualifying offer. Our fundamental intent was to generate a database of location information and user response to offers that could be analyzed to try to determine the potential power of location-derived insight. Ultimately, the results of the trial could be used to pitch the idea to advertisers.

Not everything went according to plan. The developer who was working on the application struggled with a couple of tricky components, creating schedule risk. Despite careful efforts to manage privacy concerns, one potential customer threatened a lawsuit. The location data that came in was messy and hard to analyze. Some customers engaged in the pilot; others didn't. Finding customers quickly and cost-effectively without tapping into AsiaCom's database (for a variety of reasons, the test had no public connection to AsiaCom) proved challenging.

To handle these challenges, the small, fully dedicated team had a daily "scrum" to triage critical problems. They weren't afraid to make big changes in real time to make sure they achieved their critical learning objectives. For example, every day they experimented with new ways to engage customers. Finding simple ways to get people to take action (one memorable idea involved offering a dollar to people who sent in a picture of something that made them smile on a rainy day) led to long-term increases in engagement. The team kept careful notes of both expected learning (being transparent mitigated privacy concerns) and unexpected surprises (most databases of so-called points of interest in a city were built for car navigation, which made them less than ideal for more personal services). A select group of AsiaCom senior leaders reviewed these findings in both informal and formal review settings. Some actively participated in the trial, downloading the application and using it themselves.

After three months, AsiaCom's confidence in key assumptions had increased. It also had a more grounded view of what it would take to develop and scale the business—which, given its complexity, was quite a lot! In the

TABLE 5-1

AsiaCom's fit with principles of successful experiment design

Small, focused teams	Four-person, fully dedicated core team focused on critical assumptions related to creating unique insight, consumer response, and privacy concerns
Careful design	Creation of detailed experiment plan with specific predictions for each test
Aim to learn in market	Real data generated using custom-created mobile phone app
Maximize flexibility	Staged investment, use of outside vendors for "good enough" product design
Savor surprises	Key executives participated directly in the test
Act based on learning	Significant redesigns between the alpha and beta test, decision to invest after test

project's final phase, a team of internal data scientists analyzed the data to infer patterns that predicted behavior. Through a mix of art and science, the team identified a number of powerful insights, supporting significant investments in the category. As of the writing of this book, revenue growth is outpacing initial internal projections, and AsiaCom appears to be well in front of its peers in the space.

Table 5-1 shows how AsiaCom fit the principles of successful experiment design.

Key Messages from This Chapter

1. Keep the team lean to ensure focus on a small number of variables.

2. Carefully design the experiment by having a *h*ypothesis, setting test *o*bjectives, making *p*redictions, and developing a detailed *e*xecution plan (HOPE).

3. Maximize flexibility by tapping into low-cost external resources.

4. Savor the surprising results and make adjustments (including potentially shutting down the project) based on learning.

CHAPTER 6

The Experiment Cookbook

For centuries, man looked up in the sky and wondered, "What if . . .?" If birds could fly, surely there was a way for humans to take to the air as well. How did would-be aviators test their assumptions? Most built a version of their solution, went to a high place, and jumped. Incorrect assumptions had predictable results. The industrial revolution opened up new possibilities, so by the late nineteenth century, tinkerers around the world began building physical prototypes of mechanical solutions, dedicating years of their lives to creating machines that frustratingly kept failing.

The way the Wright brothers approached the problem is instructive for innovators contemplating how to progress their ideas through the first mile. Rather than going to the top of a tall building and jumping or spending years tinkering to create the perfect prototype, the Wright brothers built and flew kites. Not only could they build kites more rapidly, but when it turned out that a particular wing design didn't work in certain conditions, they hadn't risked life and limb or emptied their bank accounts to gain that learning.

In 1901 they found another way to test assumptions quickly and cheaply. Using a wooden box, a hacksaw blade, bicycle-spoke wire, and a fan, they built a six-foot-long wind tunnel. It allowed them to see how differently shaped wings would perform in different wind conditions without having to build an entire craft that they would have to rebuild if something bad happened.

In two exhilarating months, the Wright brothers tested more than two hundred wing designs. They experimented with models proposed by other would-be aviators, carefully measuring the aerodynamic lift of different wings in different wind conditions. Wilbur Wright later recalled that they learned that most of the mathematical assumptions inventors used about how different aspect ratios—the ratio between the wing's length and span—would affect lift were "full of errors."

Kites and wind tunnels allowed the Wright brothers to learn a tremendous amount without taking undue risk or spending too much, helping them create the craft that completed the first manned flight in 1903 and ushered in the modern age of aviation. As Wilbur Wright later noted, "Sometimes the non-glamorous lab work is absolutely crucial to the success of a project."

So innovators standing at the start of the first mile should look for the business equivalent of a wind tunnel—mechanisms to gain confidence in critical areas of uncertainty in resource-efficient ways.

This chapter specifically focuses on fourteen discrete "recipes" in Innosight's experiment cookbook, organized by the rough amount of time and effort they take to execute (note, four of these recipes are financial approaches that were discussed in chapter 3). Table 6-1 summarizes these experiments, providing keys to success, and watch-outs. Figure 6-1 plots these tests on the first mile certainty table to approximately match the experiments with the level of knowledge in each key area of a new idea.

If You Have Hours . . .

It might seem impossible to address critical uncertainties in just a few hours. But there are eight ways to rapidly increase knowledge around key components of an idea.

1. Conduct Desk Research

While the overwhelming bias of this book is to make innovation a practical (rather than an academic) exercise, some critical uncertainties can be knocked off by straightforward desk research. Start by building grounding about the essence of the idea. What is the closest alternative to the idea you are considering? Then consider the following sources of information to learn more about key uncertainties:

- **S-1 and 10-K filings:** When a company plans to issue stock to the public, it files a very detailed report that explains key areas of its business. This *S-1 form* can

TABLE 6-1

The experiment cookbook

Experiment	How it builds knowledge	Keys to success
1. Conduct desk research.	Identifies other areas where customers are spending time/money, technologies that can unlock a market, and business model insight from comparable efforts	• Consider multiple sources. • Find ways to connect directly to experts or potential customers. • Analyze comparable public or to-be-public companies. • Follow the footnotes—look at references and connections.
2. Run a thought experiment.	Identifies hidden rate-limiting assumptions, operational risks, or potential competitive response	• Involve external participants to get fresh perspectives. • Use projection techniques—either view the world through another person's eyes or imagine a future condition. • Dream of what ultimate success would look like, then walk back to today ("shrimp stress test").
3. Build a back-of-the-envelope 4P model.	Provides a quick sanity check around key financial and operational assumptions	• Define the target market as narrowly as possible (not "if we got $1 from every person in India"). • Research analogies to gain greater confidence in assumptions around pricing and purchase frequency.
4. Make a phone call.	Provides grounding around operational assumptions and information around how others tackled similar problems	• Use modern social networking solutions. • Don't be afraid to cold-call someone—people love to talk about their area of expertise. • Ask people whom else they recommend speaking to.
5. Walk through a transaction.	Simple way to identify business model weakness (e.g., unmotivated sales channel)	• Consider the perspectives of all stakeholders. • Use other experiments to increase confidence that elements like unit costs and payments to distribution partners are grounded in reality.

6. Build a MacGyver prototype.	Increases confidence in feasibility, provides early read on production costs, and creates material to share with customers in experiments 7 and 11–14	• Don't worry about aesthetics; avoid endless tinkering to get it "just right." • Try multiple methods (e.g., drawing, web mock-up), with a focus on spending as little as possible (<$1,000). • Avoid getting fixated on a single approach—keep it rough so you don't fall in love with something that's going to change.
7. Talk to potential customers.	Provides direct feedback from customers on the idea and indirect learning about operational issues	• Bring supporting material—ideally a "MacGyver prototype" and an advertisement/brochure. • Don't be worried about reaching a statistically significant population. • Don't overreact to either positive or negative feedback.
8. Build a reverse income statement.	Surfaces key operational uncertainties and pinpoints most critical financial assumptions	• Ensure alignment around "root" of the tree (desired revenue, profit, etc.). • Have no more than three "sub" assumptions for any area—there will be more, but try to keep it simple. • Drive deep enough to surface operational assumptions (e.g., number of salespeople, manufacturing facilities, customer support representatives).
9. Run a focused feasibility test.	Provides market-grounded information about a key operational assumption	• Focus, focus, focus—be as specific as possible about the unknown that is being addressed. • Embrace the "good enough" principle—the goal isn't to scale a business but to learn if it *could* be scaled. • Get as close to the market as possible.
10. Build a detailed financial model.	Pinpoints most critical financial assumptions	• Be as comprehensive as possible . . . • . . . but don't fall into the trap of assuming that an awesome spreadsheet is an awesome business. • Ground financial assumptions in the best available internal research and comparable analysis.

(*continued*)

TABLE 6-1

The experiment cookbook (*continued*)

Experiment	How it builds knowledge	Keys to success
11. Prototype the purchase experience.	Provides rich insight into operational assumptions and furthers understanding of drivers of purchase, customer consideration set, and more	• Optimize around learning, not revenue. • Embrace creative mechanisms, such as using competitors' products. • Ensure that there are means (e.g., customer diaries) to gather feedback on both the purchase process and the postpurchase use.
12. Prototype the business model.	Develops richer view of economic viability of the business model while surfacing "unknown unknowns" that appear only when an interdependent business model is put together	• Ensure that you have sufficient scale to learn about key business model elements. • Isolate learning on critical business model unknowns to minimize investment and risk.
13. Run a small-base usage test.	Provides learning around what happens with repeated use	• Create multiple mechanisms to learn about consumer use (diaries, web surveys, discussion groups, etc.). • Focus primarily on use to avoid overloading the test and obscuring key learning.
14. Conduct an operational pilot.	Identifies what it takes to maximize customer demand, optimize delivery model, and fine-tune key business model elements	• Seek to mirror the planned scale business as much as possible to maximize learning. • Ensure that you have exhausted other mechanisms to learn, given relatively high levels of investment and risk.

FIGURE 6-1

Mapping experiments to the first mile certainty table

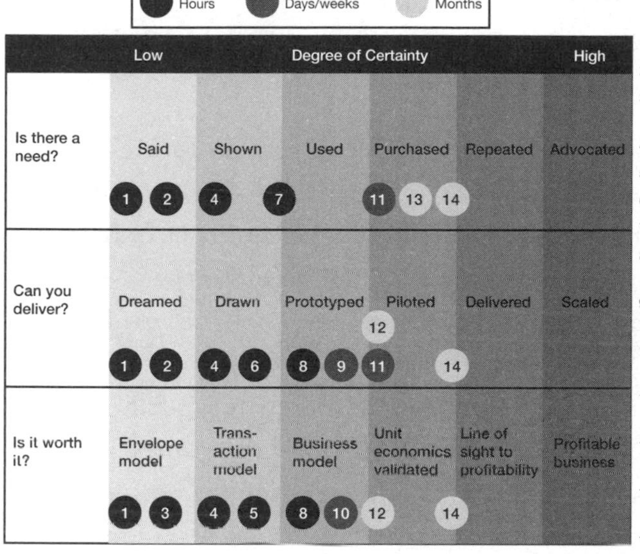

1. Conduct desk research.
2. Run a thought experiment.
3. Build a back-of-the-envelope 4P model.
4. Make a phone call.
5. Walk through a transaction.
6. Build a MacGyver prototype.
7. Talk to potential customers.
8. Build a reverse income statement.
9. Run a focused feasibility test.
10. Build a detailed financial model.
11. Prototype the purchase experience.
12. Prototype the business model.
13. Run a small-base usage test.
14. Conduct an operational pilot.

be a rich source of information about a company's business model and is easily accessible via multiple websites, including that of the US Securities and Exchange Commission (www.sec.gov). Similarly, the regular *10-K filing* a publicly traded company makes with the SEC often contains many useful details. Clearly, companies have incentives to not reveal everything about their business, but there's a wealth of information for those who are interested.[1]

1. The Jumpstart Our Business Startups (JOBS) Act passed in 2012 now allows certain companies to file draft S-1s confidentially, protecting competitively sensitive information for a period of time.

- Analyst calls: Publicly traded companies have discussions with analysts who cover their stock on a quarterly basis. Websites like seekingalpha.com provide freely available transcripts within hours of these calls, which can again provide rich information about a company or space.

- Patent filings: Not sure what a competitor's future moves are? Its patents can provide a good clue. For example, analysts had a pretty good sense as to what Apple's iPad product would look like years before its release due to the patent filings Apple had made around critical design and usability elements. Not everything that a company files will come to fruition, but it is worth a look. Specialist companies like Sagentia provide sophisticated services that perform semantic analysis on patent filings to get deeper insight into potential developments in a market space.

- Answer sites: Over the past few years, Quora and related sites have turned into excellent resources for people looking for the inside scoop about a company or a business model. If you can't find the answer, pose a question. Experts love to share their stories and will provide wonderfully rich "behind the scenes" stories about their business.

- Venture capital investments: *All the President's Men* is a gripping account of how Bob Woodward and Carl Bernstein covered the Watergate scandal that ultimately led President Richard Nixon to resign. A memorable line from the source that they code-named "deep throat"—"Follow the money"—holds true here too. Identify a hot start-up in the space. Use TechCrunch's CrunchBase database to determine its investors. See what other companies those companies have backed. If you follow the money, you can get a good sense about how a market or technology could develop.

2. Run a Thought Experiment

Fast-food giant McDonald's regularly evaluates new concepts for its menu. A few years ago, it considered a shrimp salad. The idea fit general trends toward health consciousness. It could be prepacked, fitting neatly into McDonald's delivery model. However, any idea McDonald's introduces has to have the potential to scale to its thousands of stores around the globe. McDonald's ran a thought experiment. How much shrimp would be required if it scaled the idea around the world? How did that compare with the current supply of shrimp? It turned out that McDonald's would put a significant dent in the US shrimp supply, which would drive up prices and make the idea unprofitable. You can run your own "shrimp stress test" in your imagination. What would it look like if you succeeded? Is there a hidden rate-limiting assumption that would make success impossible?

A popular exercise that originated in the military—war games—serves as a form of thought experiment. War games essentially involve simulating how combatants might respond to various tactics. In the business world, it involves putting yourself into the shoes of current and potential competitors and imagining how they might respond to your idea. War games can also be run to assess the degree to which *internal* forces might react to an idea. Consider the example of Dow Corning's Xiameter, which was detailed in Mark Johnson's *Seizing the White Space.* Johnson describes how the chemical company was evaluating a web-based distribution channel for its silicone products. Under the guidance of project leader Don Sheets (who ultimately became the company's chief financial officer), a team considered what would happen if Dow Corning tried to launch the new web business within the mainstream organization. As Johnson wrote: "The new model got crushed. It was too foreign to Dow Corning's current modes of working. The way forward became clear. The new venture would need to be free from the core business model if it was going to thrive."

Thought experiments are wonderful ways to learn because they don't cost anything and force you to take an external perspective on key strategic issues. They can be conducted by an individual, but work best when they involve a small group that has diverse perspectives.

3. Build a Back-of-the-Envelope 4P Model

As chapter 3 describes, a 4P model is a simple calculation that provides rich insight into a potential opportunity. Start by asserting the desired size of any new opportunity. Then multiply together the addressable *population*, the *purchase frequency*, and the *price* per transaction, and divide the total by the desired size to determine the required *penetration* to hit your target.

4. Make a Phone Call

A few years ago, a company that historically sold through mass-market retailers had an idea that targeted universities. The specific offering was a beverage dispenser. Under the code name Scholar, the company planned to dispense the device to centralized points on college campuses. Ample use would lead to scores of sales of the consumable components that provided the company's real profits. The plan looked great on paper (they always look great on paper). One unknown, however, was the sales cycle within universities. The team assumed that it would take about three months to work through the process of getting approval to sell to a school. However, no one on the team had ever sold to a school before. They could, of course, go and pilot the idea at a few schools and see how long it took. Or they could simply pick up the phone and call someone who made a living selling to schools. One of the team members had a family friend who worked at a company that sold security solutions to schools. He was more than happy to talk about his experiences. It turned out in many cases, the sales cycle wasn't three months—it was three *years*. Schools move slowly, with decision-making authority intentionally diffused. A beverage dispenser cut across multiple fiefdoms, meaning a three-month sales cycle was very unlikely. That didn't mean that the idea was bad, but the learning from a simple phone call led to a more realistic view about how quickly revenues would ramp up.

In my experience, people are very willing to talk about their area of expertise. And there are, increasingly, tools to find the right expert. For example, over the course of the past ten years, LinkedIn has built a network of close to 200 million people who freely share information about their career and professional interests. Find someone who has worked on something that is similar to what you are seeking to do. Connect with that person to pick his or her brain. People are generally flattered that someone took the time to find them and will be generous with their time. Another option is the more sophisticated (and more expensive) expert matching services like the Gerson Lehrman Group that have thousands of qualified experts available on demand.

5. Walk through a Transaction

Peter Drucker famously wrote that the purpose of a business is to create a customer. But that's not enough. That customer has to directly or indirectly translate into revenues. And those revenues have to be sufficient to support the costs required to deliver the product or service. One simple way to begin to test an idea's economic viability is to think with some degree about specifically how you will earn your first dollar, euro, peso, or rupee of revenue. Ask the following questions:

- How will the customers obtain the product or service?
- When will they pay for it (if at all)? And if they don't pay for it, who might (e.g., parents on behalf of kids, or advertisers on behalf of readers)?
- Where will the customers obtain it? If at third-party retailers, what do those retailers have to receive to make it in their best interests to push the product?
- How will the product or service get to the customer? If it is through a third-party distributor, what remuneration will the distributor require?
- Is there anyone else who will get a piece of a transaction (e.g., licensing fee, inventor royalty)?

This approach can highlight a weak link in an idea. For example, the amount required to motivate a sales partner might make something either too expensive for a consumer or unprofitable. Better to find those weak links as early as possible!

6. Build a MacGyver Prototype

Prototypes are a critical mechanism to speed through the first mile. By making an idea tangible, prototypes facilitate gathering valuable marketplace feedback. Over the last few decades, the design community has introduced the phrase "rapid prototyping" to the business world. The idea is to focus on speed rather than ascetics. The Apollo 13 space mission demonstrates rapid prototyping in action. Two hundred thousand miles from Earth, an oxygen tank explosion forced the astronauts to abort their mission and seek to return to Earth in the lunar module. However, the lunar module wasn't designed to sustain a crew for the length of time required. One particular deficiency was lack of a system to remove toxic carbon dioxide. The command module had lithium hydroxide canisters, but they did not naturally fit lunar module systems. In the movie version, mission leader Gene Kranz (played memorably by Ed Harris) instructs engineers to "invent a way to put a square peg into a round hole, rapidly." The engineers lacked the materials to make something elegant but developed something that got the job done, a jury-rigged solution that the astronauts called "the mailbox."

I call the kind of prototype created by the Apollo 13 team a *MacGyver prototype*, an homage to the hero of the eponymous 1980s TV show, who could regularly get out of a sticky situation with everyday materials, including seemingly ubiquitous duct tape. It is always worth thinking about how you can create a representation of your idea quickly without spending any material amount of money. That could mean a physical prototype from available material (recall Dorothea Koh's $1 prototype of wearable skin from chapter 2), a rough website using free tools like Wix.com, or even a drawing. In fact, the activities described in previous chapters involve developing rough prototypes of a business! The process of documenting an idea, building a financial model, or even talking about that idea can bring surprising clarity—and facilitate some of the other tests described in this chapter.

7. Talk to Potential Customers

Readers of my past work will be familiar with my sister Michelle. Over the past decade, she has explored a range of business opportunities that combine her academic training (she has a PhD in clinical psychology, with a focus on language acquisition), her experience as a teacher, and the lessons she has learned bringing up her own children. Her first business helped parents teach infants and young children to communicate using sign language. It turns out the desire to communicate develops before throat muscles, which can leave children very frustrated. Sign language allows children to express themselves and parents to understand what their children really want. As throat muscles develop, children quickly learn that talking is more efficient than signing, so they replace signs with words. With good training, children can pick up dozens of signs before they talk, and studies show they enjoy long-term IQ boosts.

My sister created a modest small business running play classes and designing supporting materials (flash cards, books, and so on). After forming a partnership with Kindermusik to create a nationwide program under the name Sign & Sing, she started thinking about her next project. She decided to focus on a growing problem in the United

States—young girls bullying other young girls. Unfortunately she could speak from personal experience, as her oldest daughter was the victim of bullying from the age of about seven. In late 2010 she released a book called *Little Girls Can Be Mean.*

In early 2011 her publisher approached her with an interesting proposition. Her book was well received and exceeded sales targets. The publisher suggested that she introduce a cut-price ebook with about 70 percent of the book's content for about 35 percent of the price. The theory was that the ebook would reach a wider customer set and stimulate demand for the full book.

Should she do it? she wondered. On the one hand, she wanted to reach as wide an audience as possible to both help as many people as possible and create opportunities for speeches and build a "following" that would help with future work. On the other hand, she didn't want to trade higher-priced sales for lower-priced sales.

One thing I suggested was that she develop a quick summary of the idea and then discuss it with some potential customers (which could include friends and family). "But," she said, "that seems kind of random. I won't get statistically meaningful data from talking to just a few people." I asked her how many people she had talked to. "Well, no one," she responded. "One is an infinitely better sample than none," I said. Talking to potential customers increased her confidence that an ebook would reach a new audience, further building her following. She ultimately decided to go forward with the ebook, which sold well.

Talking to prospective customers can be a great way to learn about whether an idea connects with a customer as well as what it will really take to pull it off. Pitching an idea and answering customer questions almost always surfaces interesting learning. Make sure you bring some form of collateral to a customer meeting. Ideally, you should bring a MacGyver prototype (so people can see what it is) and an advertisement or brochure that describes the idea. The collateral helps customers visualize the idea, and the process of developing collateral helps you learn more about the idea.

8. Build a Reverse Income Statement

A reverse income statement is a very useful tool to identify both financial and operational assumptions. As chapter 3 describes, the approach starts by writing the generic profit target for a new idea on the left side of the page. Then work to the right, identifying no more than three calculations for any "branch" in the tree. Profit, for example, might break down to revenue, fixed costs, and variable costs. Revenue might break down to transactions and price per transaction. Include operational assumptions as well. For example, transactions might break down to the number of sales leads pursued and the overall success rate. Sales leads could break down into the number of leads an individual salesperson could handle and the number of salespeople. The discipline of mapping out the relationship between key variables identifies weaknesses and key strategic uncertainties.

If You Have Days or Weeks . . .

The eight tests described above help gain confidence that it is worth spending time developing a more fully fleshed out plan or investing in more complicated tests. But they typically still leave critical uncertainties unaddressed. Before jumping to an expensive pilot, consider four ways to learn in more resource-effective ways.

9. Run a Focused Feasibility Test

Many new businesses come out of personal frustration. In the 1990s, Netflix founder Reed Hastings had such a moment. He had rented the movie *Apollo 13* from his local video rental store and forgotten to return the video, racking up substantial late fees. As he told the *New York Times* in 2006, "I had a big late fee for 'Apollo 13.' It was six weeks late and I owed the video store $40 . . . I had misplaced the cassette. It was all my fault. I didn't want to tell my wife about it. And I said to myself, 'I'm going to compromise the integrity of my marriage over a late fee?' Later, on my way to the gym, I realized they had a much better business model. You could pay $30 or $40 a month and work out as little or as much as you wanted."

Actually, the first idea Hastings commercialized was essentially a mail-order replica of the video store model (Netflix's simple all-you-can-rent subscription model would come later). Customers would still pay late fees—after all, that enticement to return videos helped ensure adequate inventory of movies—but the ease of dropping a DVD in the mail would increase convenience and customer satisfaction. Ultimately Hastings and his team built an incredibly sophisticated system to manage the intricacies of delivering millions of DVDs around the United States, shifted to a subscription model that proved to be highly disruptive to Blockbuster and other video rental stores, and then introduced an online streaming service that involved no physical distribution at all. Before making any investment, however, Hastings had a basic question: *Could you actually mail a DVD and not have it get mangled*? It was simple enough to learn more about this uncertainty. Hastings mailed a CD to himself in an envelope. A couple of days later, he had his answer: the postal service could in fact complete a delivery without damage. Total investment: less than $5.

This is called a *focused feasibility test* because it attempts to increase certainty about a single key operational element instead of multiple areas simultaneously. There are a number of online tools that can help run these kinds of tests. For example, InnoCentive, a spin-off of pharmaceutical company Eli Lilly, makes a market between individual scientists and companies. Posting a challenge on the website can be a way to increase confidence in the technological feasibility of an idea. If no one steps up to respond to the challenge, it might be a sign that there is in fact a technological hurdle that will be difficult to overcome. Conversely, if someone delivers a solution, there goes the uncertainty.

10. Build a Detailed Financial Model

As chapter 3 cautions, don't treat financial models as gospel. Nonetheless, the process of developing the holy trinity of business—an income statement, a balance sheet, and a cash flow statement—forces innovators to sharpen their thinking about the nuts and bolts of their ideas. This activity is in the "days and weeks" category because a detailed financial model should be grounded in robust research and should go through several iterations. Remember that the model is simply a mathematical summary of assumptions, so pay more attention to the assumptions than the ultimate answer. Run "what if" analyses to identify the most critical ones, and use the output to inform other experiments.

11. Prototype the Purchase Experience

People often associate prototyping with physical products, but since the ultimate point of a commercial innovation is to earn revenue and profits, it is worth also considering how to prototype key elements of the business model. The purchasing experience in particular offers rich insight into the depth of the target customer need, other elements in the customer's consideration set, the mechanics of motivating and consummating purchase, and more.

Consider the learning a toy company received when it experimented with a new distribution channel. Over the last few years, a number of retailers have experimented with very small format vending machines. For example, a number of airports, bus stations, train stations, and highway rest stops in the United States now have Best Buy kiosks, where travelers can pick up replacement plugs for their laptops, new earphones for their portable music players, GPS devices, and more. The combination of relatively small products and relatively high prices makes the machines an attractive proposition for Best Buy.

What if, the toy company wondered, instead of simply selling our toys to retailers, we created a similar concept where we could sell games, action figures, and more? In particular, the company was interested in bringing a kiosk to hospitals. Parents often end up at hospitals for unexpected reasons and have to spend hours without their usual tools to entertain children. The company naturally had questions about the merchandise to include in a machine and the consumer attractiveness of the proposition. In a few weeks, an Innosight team designed a means to simulate the purchase experience. It involved four components:

1. A tablet computer with a simple application that mimicked what customers would experience at the kiosk
2. An LCD monitor that showed a looping PowerPoint presentation with product images
3. A range of products on a table
4. Alasdair (an Innosight principal who led the effort), who received the "order" from the tablet via a text message and "fulfilled" the purchase by taking inventory from the table

The test cost less than $1,000 and gave the company rich learning around many of its key uncertainties. Specifically, tepid demand led the company to scupper the idea. Far better to make that decision after a $1,000 investment instead of a $1 million one!

Another name for this type of experiment is a *transaction test.* One company that has embraced the notion of transaction tests in recent years is Procter & Gamble. Historically, the company had followed a rigorous research-based approach to determine the potential of an idea. The approach essentially involved having a statistically meaningful sample of consumers react to a concept. Sometimes P&G would give consumers the product to use for a few weeks before issuing surveys; sometimes consumers would simple read a written description of an idea. Sophisticated models that compared research results with comparable concepts allowed P&G to quite accurately forecast new product revenues. However, as P&G sought to improve its ability to launch new brands and business models, it recognized that this approach was less valuable with novel concepts. Consumers might report that they would use a product even if they didn't or claim to be uninterested in something they snapped up. It wasn't that consumers were consciously seeking to delude P&G. Rather, lacking a reliable frame of reference for the new product, they didn't do a good job projecting whether and how they would actually use it.

So P&G decided to follow a different approach. Teams would create small batches of products and bring them to P&G cafeterias, the company store, or even to amusement parks or malls. Following the mantra "make a little, sell a little," the goal wasn't to earn big revenues. Rather, it was to give the team learning about what part of the "pitch" of an idea really resonated with consumers. What did people react to? What led them to refer something to friends? What led to lack of interest? What made them come back? Then, of course, they could see what happened when the consumer took the product home and actually used it.

P&G could get quite creative about this process. For example, in 2008 we were working with a team that was developing a breakthrough technological platform that would bring a popular skin-care treatment from a specialized spa to a person's home. Unfortunately, the technology was still years away from being ready for use outside a laboratory. Some specialized companies, however, had introduced directionally similar (but less effective) products in the market. P&G decided to purchase a few competitive products and use them as the basis for a transaction test. Not only did the test give the team more confidence that they were working on a deep need, it showed them that the competitive solutions seemed to be perfectly adequate to delight consumers. Instead of working for years on a proprietary solution, they could license the technology and use P&G's skills in branding and scaling ideas to make a small idea big.

If You Have Months . . .

Typically, the tests described previously drive innovators toward the middle of the first mile certainty table. The idea seems to be feasible. Customers have experienced a version of the idea and seem to like it. The numbers are hanging together. It can be tempting at this stage to make major investments and accelerate progress. Be careful. Academics often contrast so-called *targeted* experiments and *integrated* experiments. Most of the tests described earlier are targeted in that they seek to address a single key unknown. Sometimes, however, unknowns are interrelated, or can be addressed only through an integrated experiment that addresses multiple elements at once. The following final experiments do just that—they essentially run mini versions of the business either to validate the results of the smaller experiments done to date and unearth a new, more viable path forward or to show that an idea isn't worth pursuing.

12. Prototype the Business Model

The first type of integrated experiment focuses specifically on key elements of the business model, namely whether an idea will create value for a customer and whether the proposed way to deliver that value is feasible. A so-called business model prototype doesn't worry about developing the systems to scale a business. Rather, it focuses on showing how the pieces of a business model could fit together to see if it is worth scaling.

Consider how Kraft Foods tested a novel business model a few years ago. At the time, the 110-year-old company housed some of the world's most venerated food brands, such as Oreo branded cookies and snacks, Kraft Macaroni & Cheese, and Oscar Mayer lunch meat (a few years after this case study, Kraft split in two, with Mondelēz International picking up Kraft's snack brands, including Oreo, the Milka and Cadbury chocolate brands, and Trident gum).

In 2009, Kraft had identified a problem. While consumers who had grown up in the 1950s and 1960s loved Kraft products, those who had grown up in the 1970s and beyond had drifted away from many of its brands.[2] With many of those brands facing dimming growth prospects, Kraft sought to find new ways to connect to this large group of customers. It asked David Bardach and Nancy Fitzgerald, part of an internal innovation team, to understand the habits of the group it dubbed "GenNow" and develop innovative growth strategies.

The team's shepherd was Bob Lowe, a thirty-year Kraft veteran. Under his guidance, they did the things common to teams in countless corporations faced with similar mandates. They conducted market research to understand habits, practices, and preferences of this group. They hired a specialist consulting agency (Innosight) to provide both capacity and capabilities. They held multifunctional brainstorming sessions that included eclectic participants such as a chef and a nutritionist. They whittled a long list of ideas down to a half-dozen and developed more detailed business cases around the lead ideas.

Then the team did something dramatically different. They bought a truck. And started selling pizza.

2. Not all had. Our five-year-old daughter swears that Kraft Macaroni & Cheese is the finest food in the world. It is hard to argue with that viewpoint.

Step back to May 2009. One of the intriguing ideas the team was exploring was called "Mobile Morsels." Research had revealed that many consumers found lunchtime to be frustrating. They worked in corporate parks with bland food choices. They didn't have enough time to drive to higher-quality restaurants. Besides, those restaurants would stretch budgets feeling the weight of the ongoing economic downturn. Bringing lunch in a brown paper bag felt like a cop-out too.

What if, the team wondered, we brought hot, delicious pizza to this customer? Kraft already provided pizza under its DiGiorno brand to stadiums and other food service providers. Gourmet food trucks were popping up in Boston, San Francisco, and New York. It looked to be a great intersection of a core brand, an emerging trend, a market opportunity, and a compelling business model.

As the team put together the business case for the idea, they drew on outside analogies to bolster the case. They mocked up the idea to help build buy-in. They then worked to identify the most critical uncertainties behind success. In particular, the team worried whether:

- Consumers would find the menu concept to be exciting
- They could find sufficient locations to make the business model work
- They could navigate through a patchwork of local zoning laws

- The novelty of the concept would generate trial, repeat, and, ultimately, advocacy from consumers

Some of those assumptions could be addressed through research, but the team made the case that some could be addressed only in a pilot of the entire business model. In the review meeting with CEO Irene Rosenfeld, the team aligned on a stretch goal: earn $1 in revenue in one hundred days.

So, a few weeks later, the team found themselves in Canada looking at a truck they had sourced through every cash-strapped entrepreneur's friend: eBay. Over the next few weeks they worked to convert the truck into a high-quality branded offering (see photo). In early September they did a soft launch—offering free pizza to 175 Kraft employees—to work out the operational kinks. Then, the second week of September, they took the next natural step—selling real pizza to real people.

As is always the case, the in-market learning increased confidence in some areas and decreased it in others. Supply chain issues, which had seemed like a big concern back in the conference rooms, proved to be relatively trivial. Consumer reaction was positive enough that Kraft could see a path to developing a lasting and compelling concept. Zoning challenges, however, proved trickier. Success would require a lot of case-by-case negotiation with local regulatory bodies. That was okay, but suggested that the concept might be better developed as a franchise business instead of a company-owned model.

Kraft's DiGiorno pizza truck

Perhaps even more importantly than the specific learning, the team learned that if they set their mind to what seemed like a ridiculous goal—earning revenue fewer than one hundred days after presenting an idea to management—they could achieve amazing things and develop rich insights into their business.

Sadly for those whose mouths are now watering and who are looking to Google the location of the nearest DiGiorno pizza truck, in 2010 Kraft sold the brand off to Nestlé, which decided not to continue the project. But the process certainly helped Kraft begin to rebuild its innovation capabilities, setting the stage for further success in 2010 and beyond under the guidance of Vice President of Breakthrough Innovation Barry Calpino.

13. Run a Small-Base Usage Test

When the most critical unknowns are around consumer behavior, it is important to get your idea into the hands of real people for some period of time. The point isn't to maximize revenue or profits but to figure out if you have found the winning combination of a compelling solution to an important problem. In some cases, gathering potential customers for an afternoon can be sufficient, but other ideas require usage over time to determine patterns of behavior, customer referral, and so on.

The difference between a business model prototype and a small-base usage test is that the former focuses more on economic assumptions, whereas the latter focuses more on end customer use.

Chapter 3 told the story of Align, the probiotic solution for irritable bowel syndrome (IBS) sufferers introduced by P&G. It was quite clear that for the business to scale, the ultimate business model would be P&G's traditional model of mass-market advertising coupled with widespread distribution through retail channels. However, given that the key uncertainty was around everyday use and repeat purchase, P&G ran an experiment through a special-purpose website called aligngi.com, where consumers could order the product. P&G worked with doctors in three US cities to stimulate demand. Word began to spread in online communities populated by IBS sufferers, and within a few months orders had come in from almost every US state.

Direct distribution allowed P&G to regularly engage with consumers via online forums and diaries to learn more about usage frequency, repeat purchase, and more. Not only did this experiment increase confidence that P&G had a big idea on its hands, it provided useful learning about packaging, branding, and communicating with the consumer. For example, consumers had to take the product every day for it to be effective, and a few told P&G they couldn't always remember if they had taken the pill or not. P&G modified packaging so that pills were in a simple blister pack that had the days of the week on it, making it much easier for consumers to stay on track.

14. Conduct an Operational Pilot

While the previous experiments were about focused learning, an operational pilot is meant to essentially be a small-scale version of the envisioned business. It is a fully integrated experiment, with a goal of developing a plan to launch and scale a business. Operational pilots can be quite complicated. For example, in 2011, Innosight worked with medical device manufacturer Medtronic to pilot a new business model in India. This business model sought to address a fundamental challenge: India has more heart disease than any country in the world, yet the penetration of Medtronic's flagship pacemaker product was astonishingly low. We zeroed in on two root causes of low penetration:

- Lack of awareness: A lack of robust primary care meant that many patients didn't know that a pacemaker could address symptoms like weakness and dizziness.

- **Unaffordability:** Most Indians pay directly for health care. Medtronic's basic pacemaker cost about $1,000, placing it out of reach of most customers.

We called the program "Healthy Heart for All." It involved an innovative combination of direct marketing (leaflets, billboards, and websites), diagnostic camps where technicians would use low-cost electrocardiogram machines to screen dozens of people in an afternoon and wirelessly send their ECGs to be read by doctors hundreds of miles away, changes to the supply chain to lower the costs select hospitals would pay for pacemakers, and India's first financing plan for medical devices.[3]

In 2011 we launched pilots in partnership with three hospitals in India. The goal was to see whether these efforts would lead to material increases in pacemaker implants and to see if the novel financing program was commercially feasible. The hospitals we selected were in different geographies to allow for cross-comparison. The pilots provided rich learning around the ideal mix of awareness-generating techniques, how to best select and work with hospitals, and mastering the operational complexity of the financing scheme. In 2012 the pilots screened twenty thousand patients and led to two thousand pacemaker implants.

---

3. Think about that for a minute. If you get a loan for a house and don't pay it back, the bank repossesses the house. If you get a loan for an implantable medical device and don't pay it back . . .

In mid-2012, Medtronic CEO Omar Ishrak told investment analysts that pilot hospitals saw pacemaker implants double. Based on the positive results, Medtronic decided to scale the program across India and potentially to other markets as well. As of the writing of this book, hundreds of loans had been granted without Medtronic suffering a single default.

Operational pilots bear strong similarities to business model prototypes. However, they typically involve more investment because they really are subscale versions of the envisioned business rather than controlled efforts to learn about the business model. That also makes operational pilots riskier. As such, ideally they should be run when you are reasonably confident that you have a viable opportunity and you are seeking to learn how to optimize that opportunity when you launch it.

Key Messages from This Chapter

1. There are many different ways to learn about an idea.
2. Match the test with the biggest strategic uncertainty behind your ideas.
3. Keep things as simple as possible—many valuable tests can be done in just a few hours.

PART I SUMMARY

The First Mile Readiness Checklist

Are you ready to confidently confront innovation's first mile? Use the following fourteen items as a checklist that assesses the degree to which you have put the ideas in this book's first section into practice:

DOCUMENT YOUR IDEA

1. Our idea is clearly and comprehensively documented.
2. Visuals and stories help bring our idea to life.

EVALUATE IT FROM MULTIPLE ANGLES

3. We have clearly defined success criteria.
4. We have evaluated our idea against qualitative patterns of success.
5. We have determined key financial assumptions by reverse-engineering financials.

FOCUS ON THE MOST CRITICAL STRATEGIC UNCERTAINTIES

6. We have a running list of uncertainties.
7. We have short-listed deal-killing and other focus uncertainties.

TEST RIGOROUSLY AND ADAPT QUICKLY

8. We look for wind tunnels—resource-efficient ways to learn about key unknowns.
9. Our learning team is small, focused, and appropriately skilled.
10. Our test plan has clear hypotheses, objectives, and predictions and detailed execution plans.
11. We will have a bias to action and be market-oriented in our approach to learning.
12. We plan to embrace conscious constraints to speed learning and preserve flexibility.
13. We have predetermined milestone meetings already set up.
14. We will be open to all options, including pivoting or shutting down.

The following figure maps these fourteen items to the four parts of the DEFT process and also highlights the key tools to use along the way.

Overview of the first mile toolkit and checklist

- Clear and comprehensive documentation
- Visuals and stories to bring ideas to life

- Defined success criteria
- Idea evaluated against qualitative patterns
- Financial uncertainties generated by reverse-engineered financials

- Running list of uncertainties
- Short-listed deal killers and path dependencies

- Use resource-efficient wind tunnels for learning
- Small, focused, skilled learning team
- Plan with hypothesis, objectives, predictions, and execution plan

- Bias to action in learning
- Conscious constraints to preserve flexibility
- Predetermined milestone meetings
- Open to pivoting and shutting down

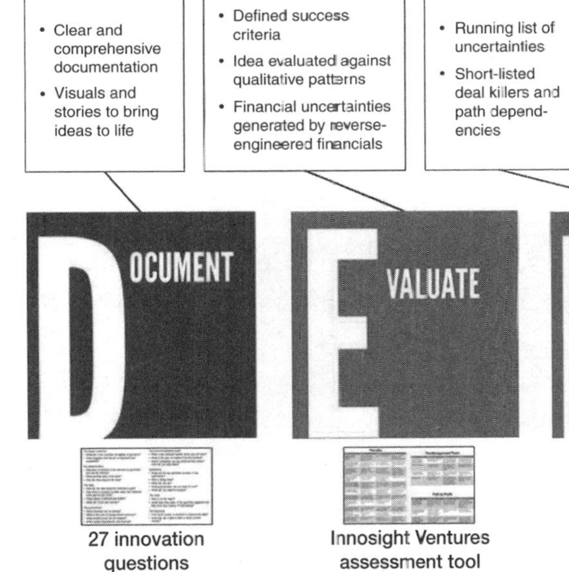

27 innovation questions

Idea resume

Innosight Ventures assessment tool

Reverse income statement

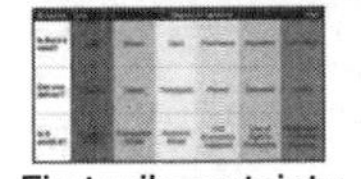

First mile certainty table

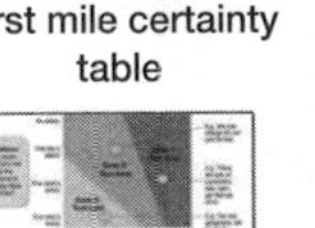

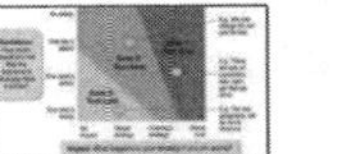

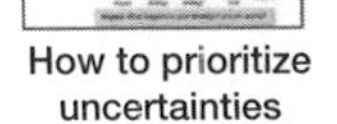

How to prioritize uncertainties

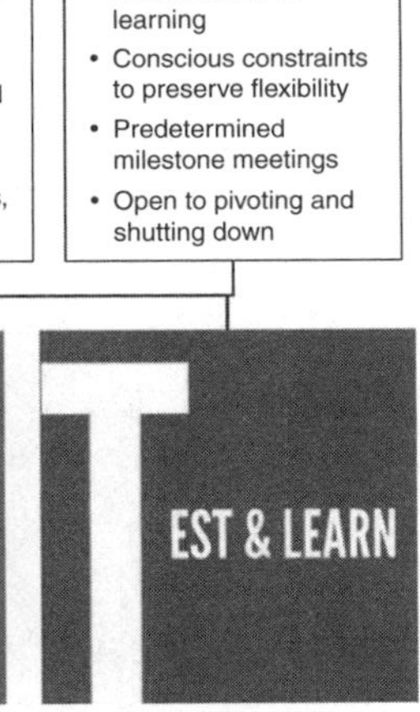

HOPE template

Experiment cookbook

PART II

Overcoming First Mile Challenges

While the DEFT process is straightforward, danger lurks in innovation's first mile. Chapter 7 describes how to overcome four common challenges that teams—whether stand-alone start-ups or groups within massive enterprises—typically encounter. Chapter 8 looks more specifically at systems that can make strategic experimentation less of an unnatural act at large companies whose primary purpose is to execute today's model. Finally, chapter 9 details advice for leaders looking to build their ability to grapple with the unfamiliar challenges they will face in innovation's first mile—or any situation characterized by high degrees of ambiguity.

CHAPTER 7

Overcoming Four First Mile Challenges

Every day, just about all of us risk our lives, even if we don't realize it. That moment comes when we get into an automobile. Despite efforts to make cars safer and improved road conditions, each year more than a million people globally die in automobile accidents. Here's one way to frame the dangers that still exist on our roads. The September 11, 2001, terrorist attacks are seared into the American and, indeed, global consciousness. About three thousand people died in the attacks on the World Trade Center, the Pentagon, and on United Airlines flight 93, which crashed in Pennsylvania. The nation's air-travel system was shut down for two days, and fear of flying led many people to eschew airplanes in favor of seemingly safer cars. A German academic estimated that shift led to an incremental sixteen hundred casualties over the next year. Dispersed events don't garner the headlines that public ones do, but that's no less horrifying a number.

Following the DEFT process rigorously acts as a kind of an airbag for innovators traversing innovation's first mile. The pages that follow describe four common challenges (summarized in table 7-1), warning signs that suggest you may have (often unintentionally) run into trouble, and tips for getting back on track. Consider this chapter your driving school and GPS system!

Challenge #1: Make a Wrong Turn

There aren't often detailed maps when it comes to innovation. That makes it perilously easy to make a wrong turn and end up in a disappointing destination. The most frequent reason that innovators make wrong turns is the lure of *fool's gold white space.*

Innovators use different colors—"white" space, "greenfield" opportunities, or "blue" oceans—to describe the (as yet) nonexistent markets that seem to hold such growth potential. It's not hard to understand the attraction of these markets. After all, many of history's great growth businesses came from creating new markets, such as eBay's online auction model or Nintendo's simple Wii console. However, one of the ventures that we tried to develop showed us that, sometimes, white space exists for a reason.

Over the last few years, an interesting concept has emerged called *medical tourism.* The basic idea is simple. Many medical procedures in Asian markets like Thailand and Singapore are sharply cheaper than in markets like the

TABLE 7-1

First mile challenges

Name	Why it happens	Discussion questions
Make a wrong turn	Lured by fool's gold white space—attempting to target a seemingly attractive market that isn't	• Why hasn't someone else done this already? • Are there people who really care enough about this problem to spend money or time to address it?
Run out of fuel	Under-budget time or money due to the planning fallacy or to planning for only one course correction (when three or four are required)	• How do budget and timeline estimates compare with similar projects or projections by outside experts? • What are plans C and D once plan B doesn't quite work? • How can we manage investment to ensure there is room for future investment?
Pick the wrong driver	Having a business leader whose lack of empathy for the target market and/or relevant experiences impairs progress	• Does someone on the team have deep empathy for the target customers and their problem? • Do we have schools of experience that are pertinent to our problem or to the general challenges of building new businesses?
Spin out	Seeking to prematurely scale a business that hasn't yet gained deep traction with customers or developed a viable business model	• How frequently are customers referring the business to other customers? • How will we create economic value? • If we lose money on each transaction, how will we make it up on volume? Are there true economies of scale?

United States. And at least some hospitals in these markets are first-rate, with highly trained doctors and cutting-edge equipment. The cost difference is enough that an insurance company could provide a patient with first-class tickets and five-star accommodations, cover the medical procedure, and still come out ahead. We formed a joint venture with Singapore's Ministry of Health to develop the business, with a particular focus on attracting patients from the United States. We hired a highly qualified health-care expert to lead the business. The business sounded great, the plan on paper looked stellar, and a series of in-depth interviews with benefits managers at Fortune 500 companies suggested a market need.

One team member, however, was skeptical. He wondered why someone hadn't already created a business to exploit such a seemingly obvious market.[1] As Matt Eyring and Clark Gilbert described in a useful 2010 *Harvard Business Review* article on managing risk, by running simple experiments the team:

> learned that patient demand was actually quite tepid and limited to a very narrow band of procedures, and that U.S. hospitals were willing to lower their prices—to near international levels in some cases—if patients paid cash up front. By failing to

1. This recalls the joke of the two economists who see a $100 bill lying on the floor. "Ignore it," one says to the other. "Because the market's efficient, that can't be real money or someone else would have already taken it." Sometimes it does require a fresh perspective to see great opportunities, but sometimes the $100 bill really doesn't exist.

> address their greatest risk—that no market existed for their services—in the cheapest and fastest way, the team members wasted significant resources and missed a critical opportunity to redirect their strategy to something more promising, such as a venture restricted to regional medical travel within the U.S. or travel to a close international destination like Mexico.

Unpopulated market spaces should be approached cautiously. The first question should be: Why is this space unpopulated? If a technological, regulatory, or societal shift has opened up a new opportunity space or you have a unique asset that makes an unreachable market reachable, proceed. Be wary of three other, less promising circumstances:

- A stated customer need isn't a real customer need (as discussed in chapter 4, customers lie all the time when they say they will do things that they actually won't).
- There are powerful stakeholders that can inhibit adoption of a new idea (e.g., regulators or purchasers).
- The fundamental economics of the space/idea aren't attractive (see more in challenge 4 below).

One important thought exercise is to put yourself in the shoes of the natural "owner" of the white space (if one can be identified). As Innosight Ventures partner Pete Bonee explains it, "Ask yourself the question: Why hasn't this been done before? Who are the people who might have done it? Did they try? Why did they or didn't they? If it is obvious to us, why wasn't it obvious to other smart people who had opportunities to make money? What do they know that we don't?" Of course, some people see markets before the world does, but if success is predicated purely on your superior intelligence (we see it and they don't), proceed with a degree of caution. Make sure to draw on the experiment cookbook to quickly knock off risks that derailed our medical tourism business.

Challenge #2: Run Out of Fuel

One of an innovator's biggest enemies lies in the range of biases that make individuals (and groups of individuals) less than ideal decision makers (appendix B summarizes some of these biases). A particularly pernicious first mile challenge results from what psychologist researchers call *planning fallacy.* It turns out that insiders do a particularly poor job of projecting how long projects will take and how much they will cost. The planning fallacy frequently causes innovators to run out of fuel in innovation's first mile, destined to never reach their destination.

Nobel laureates Daniel Kahneman and Amos Tversky posited the basic idea in an influential 1979 paper. As recounted in Kahneman's *Thinking, Fast and Slow* (a must-read), one study found that typical homeowners expect their home improvement projects to cost about $19,000. The average actual cost? $39,000. Despite ample available information, 90 percent of high-speed railroad projects have missed budget and passenger estimates, with an average *over*estimation of passengers of about 100 percent and *under*estimation of budget of about 50 percent. Firsthand experience doesn't help either. In fact, uninvolved outsiders often offer more realistic (if somewhat negatively biased) projections than involved experts.

Our 2009 investment in a company called Versonic demonstrates how the planning fallacy can kill a promising business. The company was developing a disruptive digital audio mixer that was significantly simpler and cheaper than models offered by industry leaders such as Harman and Euphonix. The product targeted a clear white space in the form of places that wanted the benefit of professional mixing technology but didn't have the wealth or skills to employ existing solutions. We imagined markets like hotels, restaurants, and churches. Some would-be corporate customers even expressed conceptual interest in using the system in conference rooms.

Everything looked great. The original plan called for Versonic to generate its first revenues in 2010. It turned out that a basic proof-of-concept prototype wasn't ready until the end of that year. That prototype did generate advance orders from distributors, but the company had run out of money and now needed about $1.5 million in follow-on investment to manufacture its first batch of products. That amount exceeded the maximum amount we could invest through our fund, no venture capitalist in the region had any interest in the space, and while the large corporations in the space might consider acquiring a revenue-producing business, they didn't invest in emerging ones. Without a viable source of funds, the business shut down in 2011.

Versonic's story is not unusual. My basic rule for start-ups is: "It always takes longer, and it always costs more." Innovators can use three strategies to cope with the realities of the planning fallacy:

- **Get data from comparable efforts.** If you look at the whitest-hot start-ups over the past decade, the average third-year revenue is well less than $100 million. Be cautious if your plan suggests you'll be better than the best of the best.

- **Create space for misses.** We have consistently seen that for our portfolio, companies' revenues are slower in coming and development takes longer than even worst-case scenarios. This has led to a shift in our funding strategy: we will not invest in a company unless there is a coinvestor to make sure the company has a larger window and can avoid being in perpetual fund-raising mode. As Silicon Valley author and speaker Guy Kawasaki puts it, "As a rule of thumb, when I see a projection, I add one year to delivery time and multiply revenues by 0.1."

- **Be disciplined.** Pete Bonee believes companies often "deplete their batteries" with go-to-market false starts before they have generated real traction, nailed their value proposition, or figured out their economic model. "Entrepreneurs need to have a board that forces them to get the fundamentals right first, and governs their spending to limit the battery drain in the meantime," he says. "As the saying goes, 'Nail it, then scale it.'"

Planning fallacy becomes only a bigger challenge once you recognize the reality that success typically requires at least a couple of wrong turns or false starts. Recall Steve Blank's definition of a start-up in chapter 1 as a temporary organization that is searching for a scalable business model. As Blank notes, "No business plan survives first contact with the market." That's okay as long as innovators, in the words of Blank's protégé Eric Ries, are prepared to "pivot" toward a more successful strategy. However, one lesson that we have learned is that success rarely comes from a single shift. Rather, most businesses take at least two shifts before they succeed.

Consider Innosight's investment activities. The theory behind our first efforts in 2005 was that a unique relationship with Harvard's Clayton Christensen (Innosight's cofounder and a world-recognized innovation thought leader) would afford us what the industry calls *proprietary deal flow;* that is, we would see ideas that no one else in the world would see.

We did indeed see some novel ideas. For example, in 2006 we received a business plan for Helios 2. Helios 1 is . . . the Sun. The plan stated, "The New Sun (Helios 2) Technology will avoid the problems of counterproductive competition for energy security among the traditional energy power producers and oil producing countries and restore a balance for fair energy supply which is fundamental to global energy sufficiency and stability. Helios 2 will be the second SUN with a total possible output to match the Sun's 386 billion, billion megawatts output." All it would take was $98 billion to acquire the technology. Yes, that's billion with a *b*. Clearly, we had not yet found a formula for success. We concluded that the market for start-up investment, at least in the United States, functioned reasonably efficiently.[2]

In 2007 our next round of experiments in venture investing was based on the concept that the process that formed the backbone of our consulting engagements would give us a unique ability to *create* our own ventures. While the systematic approach did surface some interesting opportunities, the small team of people who had limited experience launching new ventures struggled to compete with a gazillion entrepreneurs around the globe. We deemed this experiment too to be a commercial failure, though we were happy with the substantial learning that came from living in innovation's first mile.

2. The recent rise of Kickstarter, Indiegogo, and other "crowd-funding" platforms would present at least some evidence to the contrary, as these platforms have provided funding to thousands of artists and entrepreneurs who had been overlooked by traditional funding providers.

Finally, in 2009 we decided to ground our investment efforts in the unique way in which we *select* high-potential market spaces and *shape* rough ideas into sustainable business models (largely following the approach detailed in this book and other Innosight publications). The book isn't closed yet on this experiment, but by all accounts it seems to be working. The third time is indeed a charm!

Idea sponsors need to accept that any idea will need to morph several times before it succeeds. This reality places a premium on starting in-market learning early rather than treating innovation like an academic exercise. The better the starting point, obviously, the less jarring the shifts, but "unknown unknowns" mean that the sooner learning starts, the better.

Challenge #3: Pick the Wrong Driver

Imagine you have spent all of your life driving a car with automatic transmission. One day you arrive at a rental car location and find out that they have only cars with manual transmissions. You consider yourself a good driver, but you are utterly unable to make the car go anywhere. Similarly, the world's very best professional drivers rarely switch from the open-wheel cars that characterize Formula One or Indy Car competitions to the types of the cars used in the NASCAR series. As innovation is an intensely human activity, having appropriate talent behind the wheel is critically important.

Ideal drivers have two characteristics: empathy for the target market and some set of relevant experiences that has prepared them innovation's first mile.

Empathy and the Thousand-Monkey Problem

Creating a business can be approached methodically. But it can be hard to have an overly clinical approach click with the market.[3] Many founders start businesses based out of a personal frustration. For example, Reed Hastings's frustration with high late fees for his failure to return a movie rental led to Netflix. Grounded empathy about customers, their problems, their desires, and their constraints is an important ingredient to developing a solution with sufficient resonance to support a scalable business.

Consider a business we started working on in 2006 called Guaranteach. The idea was ripped right out of Clayton Christensen's research on how to disrupt primary education (summarized in his 2008 book with Michael Horn and Curtis Johnson, *Disrupting Class*). Everyone learns differently, the theory goes, but everyone is taught the same way (by a teacher in front of the class). Well, our idea was to create a platform where consumers would come in and take a quiz to determine their learning preferences. We then developed a library of more than twenty thousand teacher-submitted videos.

3. There are exceptions, of course—Jeff Bezos was very careful in his choice of books as the first market for Amazon.com, and he's done just fine for himself. The first mile challenges detailed in this chapter are guidelines, not rules.

The business struggled to gain commercial traction. At least one reason was a mismatch between the experiences of the management team and the needs of the business. Guaranteach was led by two people who, on the surface, had a deep understanding of the challenges of teaching and tutoring. Both the CEO and the COO had high school teaching experience (twelve years between them), but this experience had been acquired ten years previously, in other countries, and before the internet had become commonplace.

As such, Guaranteach's leadership team didn't have truly relevant experiences that would have given them deep empathy for the challenges faced by US teachers and students in an online world. In fact, as Guaranteach COO Alasdair Trotter (who is now a consultant with Innosight) noted, "Our ten-year-old experiences were at best slightly helpful and at worst dangerously misleading. I think George [the CEO] and I (despite our protestations) never really understood what it was like to be a teacher in a US middle school—we could have done so much more in the early days to understand parent/teacher/student angst."

Corporate innovation efforts often suffer from empathy gaps. For example, a few years ago, a Fortune 100 product-based company made the strategic decision to build a service business. It was a high-profile project. The CEO was a huge believer in the effort. Industry analysts projected that the market the team was targeting would be massive, and the playing field was still wide open. The CEO gave the team significant amounts of resources. The team swelled to one hundred people over the course of a year.

Yet, eighteen months after getting started, the team still didn't have a clear view of its target customer, the business model, and so on. The project leader was baffled. "We have a really smart group of people—the team is the best and brightest within the organization," he told me. "But we just keep running into wall after wall."

I asked him for two pieces of data. The first was the number of people on the team who had successfully launched new businesses in the past. The second was the number of team members who had experience in service businesses. I wasn't surprised that the answers were "none" and "none."

I call this the *thousand-monkey problem.* The term references an old theory that if you give one thousand monkeys one thousand typewriters, eventually one of them will replicate a great novel like *War and Peace.*[4] Many companies, particularly those with promote-from-within cultures, believe that they can solve any problem. And if you give them enough time, they probably can work out the intricacies of business models that are new to them but known to the world. But the truth is, sometimes it is far better to bring in an outside expert who knows an industry or model cold. He or she can help to minimize time spent going down blind alleys.

For example, when Procter & Gamble (historically an entirely promote-from-within company) decided it

4. Apparently, actual tests of this hypothesis led to high levels of defecation and destroyed keyboards, but let's ignore that for a minute.

wanted to go into the franchise business, it set up a subsidiary called Agile Pursuits, which hired an outsider with substantial experience running franchises and bought a small company in Georgia called Carnett's Car Washes. These moves substantially boosted the company's expertise in executing franchise-based business models. It had begun quietly testing franchise-based car washes and dry cleaners in 2008. In 2010 it expanded the dry-cleaner business nationally. Technology companies will often follow this strategy when they execute what has been come to be called an *acqui-hire* as an effective way to access unique skills.

Too much expertise can, of course, be a problem. As Thomas Kuhn noted in *The Structure of Scientific Revolutions,* what we now call *paradigm shifts* almost by definition have to come from people outside the existing orthodoxy. Venture capitalists sometimes wait to bring in a seasoned chief executive officer to scale a company because they know that CEO will bring the business model from his or her last venture. If the company is still trying to discover its business model, that presents challenges. But all else being equal, seek drivers who know what they're doing. One who is just learning the ropes of a market filled with experts can end up languishing in the first mile.

Finding First Mile–Friendly Talent

Ideally, innovators have "schools of experience" and personalities that prepare them for the challenges they will encounter as they work on their idea. The term traces back to the 1998 book *High Flyers*, by academic Morgan McCall.

In that book, McCall argues that managers are made more than they are born. What gives a manager skills are the courses he or she takes in the schools of experience.

Beyond specific industry experience, what characterizes people who have the greatest chance of succeeding at innovation's first mile, and where can companies find that talent?

Professors Jeffrey Dyer and Hal Gregersen draw a useful distinction between "discovery" and "delivery" skills. Whereas delivery skills relate to executing against known problems, discovery skills relate to finding answers to uncertain problems. Specific discovery skills that Dyer and Gregersen highlight include:

- Questioning: Regularly adding or imposing constraints or asking simple questions such as "What if?"
- Experimenting: Trying things, sometimes just to try them
- Observing: Spending time out in the field, paying particular attention to unexpected things
- Associational thinking: Putting disparate ideas together, such as when Steve Jobs drew on inspiration from a college calligraphy class to design the look and feel of early Macintosh computers

Beyond these skills, first mile operators need to have three unique abilities:

- **Incredible detail orientation:** It's easy to associate innovation with head-in-the-cloud visionaries, but an experiment, particularly a market-facing one, can have dozens of moving pieces. A lack of attention to detail almost always leads to missed opportunities for learning.

- **Comfort with micro course corrections:** The AsiaCom team described in chapter 5 made literally hundreds of small changes to their prototype to maximize learning. Any experiment is going to run into challenges that could not have been predicted at the outset. Failing to make real-time changes will minimize learning.

- **An eye for the unexpected:** Remember, running experiments isn't purely to *confirm* preexisting notions, but also to *learn*. People with natural curiosity, who like to tear things apart and rebuild them, can spot the unexpected development that ends up providing vital learning.

How can you identify the right talent? Look for people who have interesting hobbies outside their job. See if there is anyone who has started a business at some point in his or her career. Don't worry if that business failed—the point is to find people who have experience grappling with uncertainty.

If you are in a corporation, where should you look to find this talent? It is tempting to simply outsource the problem and bring in a group of outsiders with substantial entrepreneurial experience. That approach has some risks. No company can innovate *faster* than the market in which it participates. A company can innovate *better* than the market in which it participates if it taps into some of its unique capabilities. Outsiders can struggle to develop and leverage connections with the core business. Sometimes entrepreneurs can be too entrepreneurial, leading to mutual frustration and occasional chaos. A fully external team can lead to an unfortunate "us versus them" situation that inhibits progress. But since outsiders can bring in vitality and fresh perspectives, an ideal team carefully balances handpicked insiders and a select number of outsiders.

Finding the right talent inside an organization seems challenging. Start by looking for people who had roles—such as launching a new product or entering a new geography—featuring high degrees of uncertainty.[5] Then look to the organization's fringes. There might be employees who are languishing because their natural inclinations to work on discovery projects are being stifled in more execution-oriented roles.

Recognize too that the behaviors detailed earlier improve with conscious practice. Companies who want to

---

5. There are also diagnostics that determine an individual's innovation tendencies. For example, Gregersen and Dyer offer self-administered and 360-degree assessments at their website theinnovatorsdna.com. (*Note:* While Innosight has an affiliation with Gregersen and Dyer, we have no commercial tie to this tool.) An intriguing start-up called Knack is attempting to "gamify" the process of identifying and nurturing talent. It develops immersive online games. When people play the games, they display about a dozen key tendencies. By comparing an individual with broader populations of successful innovators, Knack can pinpoint different pools of talent inside an organization. (*Note:* The author has invested in Knack.)

build capabilities around learning should seek to have a full-time team that gets a chance to work on a number of different projects. It is rare for any corporate assignment to go much beyond two years these days, but providing space for repetition will increase performance and spread skills throughout the organization.

Challenge #4: Spin Out

You seem to be squarely on the road to success. You have plenty of fuel in the tank. You are confident that your leadership team is up to the task. It is natural to think that the best way to speed through innovation's first mile is to, well, speed up. Jam your foot on the virtual accelerator and build your business as quickly as possible. However, research by the Startup Genome suggests that the number-one reason new companies fail is premature scaling. That is, a company accelerates growth before it has really formed a viable business model, and it all comes crashing down. In innovation's first mile, going too fast can lead to a business spinning out of control and crashing.

The two specific issues we've seen are scaling a business that hasn't yet created a deep connection with customers and scaling a *concept* before it is a *business.*

Nail the "Wow!" Before the "How?"

It's easy to think that early website visits or revenue means you are ready to scale. But our experience suggests that without something deeper—call it *love*—early success is destined to be fleeting. As an example, consider the challenges we encountered when building Guaranteach. We certainly made progress with the idea, driving the cost per submitted videos down substantially and generating sufficient content to cover the entire K–12 math curriculum. Almost all of the figures on our comprehensive dashboard (a subset of those figures appear on table 7-2) were moving in the right direction. Confident we were on the path to success, we raised money from blue-chip players in the education space, such as the NewSchools Venture Fund and the Bill & Melinda Gates Foundation. We used the funding to develop a more robust system that we could scale to dozens, and then hundreds, of schools.

There was one small problem. Students didn't like our system, so we never really got market traction. In a memorable 2009 email, a board member noted, "I think the theory of the case is a bit flawed . . . sticky regular users would validate the concept and we haven't seen this yet." The board member was right. We sold Guaranteach in 2011 at a price tag that didn't come close to covering the capital invested in the business. Concurrently, Khan Academy—with one individual providing basic videos—took off (demonstrating that this wasn't a fool's gold white space!).

Innovators should make sure they focus on the "Wow!" before getting too obsessed with the "How?" Our dashboard tracking more than twenty different operational variables blinded us to the fact that the lack of deep customer resonance would make it hard for the business

TABLE 7-2

Guaranteach August 2009 dashboard

Area	7/6/2009	7/20/2009	8/3/2009	8/17/2009
Accepted pieces of content	107	125	138	150
New pieces last week	105	127	105	89
Active contributors	111	137	105	95
Engineering active days	104	111	116	121
Release version	*2.1*	*2.1.27*	*2.1.29*	*2.1.31*
Last month's spend	131	131	111	111
Total invested	116	116	130	130
Bank balance	29	29	325	325
Weekly web traffic	86	118	108	117
Visits from nonpaid search	83	104	202	231
Number of nonpaid search keywords	97	95	213	253
Active free trials	103	107	94	97
Free trials last week	97	101	68	87
Total paying accounts	101	108	111	135
Cumulative subscriber months	103	113	119	131
Weekly subscription revenue	67	67	100	122
Year-to-date revenue	103	113	120	163
Pilots run this week	*0*	*1*	*2*	*0*
Number of users giving feedback	*0*	*39*	*12*	*4*

Note: Figures indexed to 6/29/2009 = 100 except for raw figures in italics.

to scale (Eric Ries has a memorable term for the ultimately useless metrics we were tracking: *vanity metrics*). Innovators should make sure their measures help them understand the resonance of their idea. Are customers talking about the product or service with their friends? What are they saying? Are they passionate about it (passionate dislike is okay, because it indicates that you are targeting the right basic space)?[6]

Don't Forget the Finances

Are you working on a concept or a business? They might seem to be the same thing, but there is one big difference. A concept can be fun, exciting, intriguing, and compelling. A business, hopefully, is one or more of those things—but it also *makes money.* For the most part, while a concept might serve as a springboard, a business is the innovator's desired destination. Consider Village Laundry Service (VLS). The idea has received more press attention than any other business launched by Innosight. It has been covered in magazines, newspapers, television programs, and even featured in Eric Ries's book *The Lean Startup.* Part of this press attention springs from a very compelling story. The business was conceived by then Innosight Ventures

6. Net Promoter Score is a simple way to measure how deeply an idea resonates with a set of customers. As described in the *Harvard Business Review* article "The One Measure You Need to Grow," by Bain's Fred Reichheld, the technique involves asking customers whether they would recommend a product or service to a friend. Subtract the percentage of people who score less than 6 on a 10-point scale from the percentage of people who score a 9 or 10 and you have your answer.

partner Hari Nair.[7] The idea was to develop an attractive laundry model for India's surging middle class. The target customers faced unattractive trade-offs. They could use their local *dhobi*, who cleaned laundry for about 20 rupees per kilogram (about 33 cents at 2013 exchange rates). That was incredibly affordable, but the cleaning process, involving hand-washing in less than perfectly clean water, using harsh detergents, and removing stains by beating clothes against rocks, had some clear downsides. It also took seven to ten days to return clothes. Alternatively, the customer could use a high-end cleaning service that was much more expensive or buy an expensive washing machine and have a maid wash clothes at home.

Nair's model involved a small kiosk (see photo) staffed by a couple of attendants. The kiosks, which we dubbed "laundry rigs," would have modern washing machines, dryers, and irons. Customers would drop their laundry off and collect it twenty-four hours later. Convenience came at a price, but it was still more affordable than other higher-end options and didn't require purchasing a washing machine. Instead of viewing Village Laundry as a threat, perhaps dhobis could become franchise owners, building nice income streams for themselves. The concept of franchises was not new to India, and the well-publicized growth of a coffee chain called Café Coffee Day and Domino's Pizza had created interest in the model.

7. As of the writing of this book, Nair is the managing director of Breakthrough Innovation at Kimberly-Clark, though he remains active on the VLS board of directors.

A Village Laundry Service kiosk

VLS had a robust business plan, grounded in comparable analysis and vetted by industry experts. A quick test in late 2008 seemed to validate that the rig-based business resonated with customers and showed that operations were feasible. Over the next couple of years, VLS attracted a management team and deployed twenty rigs around Bangalore and Mysore. This allowed us to see how the system functioned at scale. It gave us more robust insight into generating demand, delivering the high-quality service that drove repeat business, managing costs, handling key operations issues, and differentiating costs that were truly tied to a single location from fixed costs that could be spread across a network of kiosks.

From late 2008 to late 2010 the business's revenues grew at a compound rate of 14 percent—*per month.* However, individual units could not consistently cover basic operating costs. This indicated a fatal flaw in the rig-based business model. There are many reasons to innovate, but at the end of the day, if a business idea isn't backed by an economically viable model, it can't be sustained. For VLS, that meant:

- A single customer transaction had to bring in more revenue than the costs incurred in delivering the service.
- A single rig had to attract enough revenue to cover manpower, rental charges, and other fixed costs.
- A collection of rigs had to generate enough operating profit to support broader overhead.

VLS crossed the first hurdle but never managed to clear the second or third. In 2011 a new management team, supported by a fresh round of outside financing, went back to the proverbial drawing board. The business shifted to a home-delivery model out of a central store. The team pushed prices still higher and offered new benefits, such as advanced stain removal. In 2012 the revised model demonstrated that it could cross the second threshold. However, as of the writing of this book, VLS still hadn't figured out the third area, raising questions about its long-term viability (though to its credit, the team perseveres!).

Innovators need to start with a deep understanding of how the business will actually make money. What is a transaction? How much does a unit cost to deliver? How much does it cost to produce? If these unit economics don't work, the odds that it ever will build a viable business model are very low. Innovators too frequently wave away these concerns saying they will solve them once they "scale." But if you can't make a single transaction work, consider whether you have really developed a business or just a concept. Businesses scale. Concepts don't.

The proper preparation and approach can help to make the first mile a less perilous place. The next chapter describes systems companies can build to help facilitate strategic experimentation.

Key Messages from This Chapter

1. It's easy to be lured by fool's gold white space and make a wrong turn in innovation's first mile.
2. Money is the fuel of innovation; the planning fallacy means that innovators too frequently run out of gas because efforts take longer and cost more than they expect.
3. The wrong driver—one who lacks empathy for a target market or pertinent skills for a given business model—can lead to stalled innovation efforts.
4. Speeding up can lead to spinning out. Make sure you have created a deep connection with customers and are working on a business, not a concept.

CHAPTER 8

Systems to Support Strategic Experimentation

While detailed data on the success rate of corporate innovation efforts is difficult to obtain, most executives agree that the overwhelming majority of their investments in growth prove disappointing.

The fundamental challenge inside most companies is that the core systems are optimized around supporting today's business model, not developing tomorrow's. Those systems act like corporate antibodies that snuff out strategic experiments—not through malice, but simply through attempting to keep the enterprise humming along without getting distracted.[1] Four specific

1. For a fun, somewhat subversive, book on this topic, read *The Innovator's Extinction*, by David Ulmer. Some of the advice in the book should be followed with caution, but Ulmer bears the scars of trying to drive innovation inside several large companies, and a lot of his observations ring all too true.

systems can inoculate the corporate innovator against these antibodies:[2]

1. Decision-making systems that pierce through the "fog of innovation"
2. Rewards systems that encourage smart risk taking and don't overly penalize failure
3. Project disengagement mechanisms that end the plague of "zombie projects"
4. Systems that foster connections to external experts, customers, and employees

This chapter describes each of these systems in depth. If you're working on a project inside a company that lacks these systems, make sure you have a senior sponsor who can help you work around the problems you're destined to encounter while you make the case for the creation of systems that will decrease the friction impeding strategic experimentation.

1. Decision-Making Systems That Pierce through the "Fog of Innovation"

Every company has mechanisms for making decisions about projects. Some companies feature very formal sys-

2. My science skills peaked in seventh-grade biology, so I'm sure I blew the metaphor there.

tems that are well documented; others have more informal systems. Regardless, every company has some way to determine which project receives funding and which doesn't, where people spend their time, which executive can access key corporate systems and which cannot, and so on.

In many companies, the default project mechanisms are *mistake minimizing*—that is, there are careful controls to ensure the company doesn't squander money. That means that organizations perform multiple layers of reviews before committing resources to a project. Decisions are largely analytical, with rigorous consideration of all alternatives. Once leadership decides to commit resources, future reviews focus on progress against commitments. Is the team on or behind schedule? Is spending meeting budget expectations? Are results consistent with projections? People who deliver against their commitments get rewarded; those who don't get punished.

The first mile challenges these systems. It's rare that the data required to make a critical decision about an innovative idea is clear. History is littered by smart people making horribly wrong calls about nascent markets. Just look at the computing industry. In the 1940s, IBM's Thomas Watson predicted that there was a world market for five computers; in the 1970s, Digital Equipment's Ken Olson said there was no reason why people would want a computer in their home; in the early 1980s, Microsoft's Bill Gates said that 640K should be enough memory for anyone.[3] It's not

3. Of the three reputed projections, Gates denies ever saying what was attributed to him, and Olson reports that he was referring to the idea of a central

really their fault. Data becomes crystal clear only when it is too late to take action on that data.

So first mile decisions are often made inside what I call the "fog of innovation." It's easy to get lost in the fog and never make any decision at all, since a risk that doesn't pan out tends to have more negative repercussions on a person's career than risks not taken.[4] However, that approach often leads to people *never* making a decision, creating room for disruptive upstarts and hungry competitors. Even worse, companies often face a mismatch between the pace of decision making and the pace of discovery. I remember distinctly a large company that proudly told me about how it got all of its most important executives to sit on an all-powerful innovation board that met every ninety days. "What if," I asked, "the day after a meeting, the team discovers its strategy needs a wholesale revision?" Silence.

It's tempting to say that there shouldn't be *any* control mechanisms for more uncertain efforts. Once you've de-

---

computer controlling the home, not a simple personal computer. See http://www.snopes.com/quotes/kenolsen.asp for more.

4. This is one of a category of problems that I call the "curse of abundance." You'd think that abundance would be a source of competitive advantage for large companies. After all, deep pockets, ample pools of talent, and patience would make innovation easier. However, too much time or money allows companies to continue to follow fatally flawed strategies for too long or create overly complicated solutions that actually overshoot customer needs. For example, resource-rich companies have the "luxury" of researching. And researching. And researching. That can be a huge benefit in known markets where precision matters. But it can be a huge deficit in unknown markets where precision is impossible. Entrepreneurs don't have the luxury of infinite research, and sometimes that works in their favor. See chapter 3 of my book *The Little Black Book of Innovation* for more.

cided to innovate, the argument goes, you should form a team, give them a check, and get out of their way. Letting chaos reign, however, carries substantial risks. Remember, most ideas emerge out of a process of trial-and-error experimentation. Without control mechanisms, teams can easily follow the wrong strategy for too long. Further, weak control systems deny a company the opportunity to redirect resources to the most promising ideas or to find creative ways to combine ideas.

There should be a discipline around managing ideas in the first mile. But it needs to be a *different* discipline from mistake-minimizing systems that govern the core business.

Consider the discipline venture capitalists impose on their investments. Venture capitalists are actively involved in the companies in which they invest. Typically, a VC will sit on the company's board and interact with management on a regular basis. If a decision needs to be made, the board can assemble in twenty-four hours. Venture capitalists carefully manage the funding process to focus entrepreneurs on the most critical issues early, tying future fund-raising rounds to achieving key milestones. It is a very different approach to funding than the typical annual budgeting cycle inside most companies. Active stakeholder involvement, a scarcity mind-set, and quick decision making ensure that venture capital–backed start-ups rarely get lost in the fog of innovation.

The military too faces the need to make decisions when information isn't clear. One doctrine taught to Marines is the so-called 70 percent rule. The goal is to get enough data so that you are 70 percent confident in your decision, and then trust your instincts. If you have less data, you are making a close-to-random decision. If you wait until the data is perfect, the opportunity to make a decision that has impact has probably passed you by.

The uncertainty that characterizes the first mile requires an approach that is *experiment-encouraging*. Such an approach has six primary features:

- It is biased toward taking action over endless studying, which often means viewing investments more as strategic options (that provide the right, but not the obligation, to invest more in the future) than as "all or none" commitments.

- Reviews happen frequently and are focused less on progress against commitments and more on learning—both anticipated and unanticipated.

- Both quantitative and qualitative data inform decision making.

- Discussion and decision making do not involve "business as usual" activities; those are handled separately (perhaps even in a physically separate location). When former Procter & Gamble chief technology officer Bruce Brown led R&D for P&G's Hair Care division, for example, he would stop meetings when it was time to review disruptive projects to get new people into the room and allow the original attendees to hit a mental "reset" button before getting down to the new business.

- Review meetings feature small groups, including one or a handful of disconnected outsiders. Ideally, members of the group have experience making decisions under uncertainty, specific experience that is pertinent to the proposed idea, or both.

- Decision makers don't just passively review details; they actively participate in experiments. Remember, the most useful findings from experiments are often unpredicted. Further, many experiments involve companies exploring new market spaces, where leaders don't have grounded intuition based on decades of market experience. Decision makers assessing a market about which they know nothing not surprisingly demand significant proof before making a decision.

Academic research supports the intuitive notion that experiment-encouraging governance mechanisms help to support the creation of breakthrough ideas. In late 2010 three academics published a paper contrasting the impact of incentives on two institutions that give grants to promising life scientists. One program, led by the National Institutes of Health (NIH), features short review cycles, predefined deliverables, and tough penalties for missing milestones. In contrast, grants from the Howard Hughes Medical Institute (HHMI) have more of a long-term focus with a stated tolerance of early failure. Perhaps not surprisingly, HHMI grant recipients produce breakthrough ideas at a statistically significantly higher rate than NIH grant recipients. They also produce more total output—but have more efforts that appear to be flops. One approach minimizes failures; the other maximizes breakthroughs.

Is the HHMI system better than the NIH one? It's a trick question—the answer depends on the strategic intent. Experiment-encouraging systems aren't better than mistake-minimizing ones. In fact, a company should have *both* systems running in parallel. Mistake-minimizing systems help to maximize resource efficiency in the core business; experiment-encouraging ones help to maximize learning in new businesses.

2. Rewards Systems That Encourage Smart Risk Taking and Don't Overly Penalize Failure

The first mile can be a tough place. Tests often don't work the way people anticipate. Sometimes teams quickly learn that the deal killer they worried about is a reality. Innovation can be a risky business, and failure certainly happens.

Most leaders intuitively get the idea that innovation will have its twists and turns, and that short-term failure can lead to long-term success. However, in most organizations there is a significant disconnect between that understanding and performance management systems. The "what gets measured gets managed" doctrine that guides most organizations is a real barrier to developing a culture where experimentation happens naturally.

Incentives systems that constrain experimentation tend to be results-oriented, focused on "hard" metrics. Companies spend an inordinate amount of time carefully setting targets or key performance indicators for managers. They then meticulously measure to determine whether a manager hit their target or fell short. People who "hit their numbers" and deliver against commitments get rewarded. Fail to do that once and you get reprimanded; fail repeatedly and you get let go. While the approach can lead to strange behaviors like "sand-bagging" targets, it generally works pretty well when a manager's skill indeed determines outcomes. However, in the first mile, people can follow the right behaviors and still have an idea that doesn't pan out because an assumption proves false. Should these people be rewarded or punished?

Michael Mauboussin has thought substantially about this problem. His 2012 book, *The Success Equation*, draws a helpful distinction between outcomes that are determined almost purely by skill and those that involve luck. Roulette, for example, is based purely on luck. There's no way to tell whether someone is a "good" roulette player, because there is no such thing. In contrast, chess is a game of almost pure skill. Generally, you know chess players are skilled because of their results. Watching them play can help you understand the nature of their skills, but it isn't necessary to assess their capabilities. Blackjack is somewhere between these two examples. Consider this circumstance. You go into a casino and see a person with a big pile of chips on the table. You watch him play a hand. He boldly hits on eighteen while the dealer is showing a six. The player draws a three, landing on the magic twenty-one. Without the hit, the dealer would have won with nineteen. You ask the player how he made his decision. Maybe he has X-ray vision or is a truly world-class card counter. He smiles and says, "I just trusted my gut. Never proves me wrong." Is this a preternaturally skilled blackjack player who warrants future investment? After all, he did what often gets rewarded in corporations—he trusted his instinct, took a bold risk, and it paid off. However, while the player got the right outcome, he got it using poor behaviors. If he generally followed that pattern over time, he'd lose money, unless he was such an adroit card counter that he knew *precisely* what card was coming.[5] If you follow simple decision rules, you can do reasonably well at blackjack. If you augment those decision rules with the mental gymnastics related to counting cards, you can beat the house. But luck can still turn against you on any given hand.

The first mile is like blackjack, hitting a baseball, or investing in a stock. You can't assess people's performance based on a single event.[6] Instead, you have to carefully

5. Or was a time traveler. A topic for another book.

6. Over time, of course, an accumulated track record demonstrates capabilities. We can be pretty sure Warren Buffett knows what he is doing or that Miguel Cabrera is a skilled baseball player. Nate Silver did show in his excel-

monitor the behaviors they follow and how they make decisions. That requires a radical rethink of rewards systems—after all, management-by-objectives advocates explicitly urge managers to *ignore* behaviors and focus only on outputs. It also requires very different behavior on the behalf of leaders, who need to make sure they spend enough time with their staff to begin to understand how they think through these kinds of problems.

Finally, in the language of innovation scholar Gerard Tellis at the Marshall School of Business at the University of Southern California, rewards systems should be "asymmetric." That is, there should be "strong incentives for successful innovation but weak penalties for failure." That's exactly *opposite* the way it works in most companies—where there are strong penalties for failure and weak rewards for success!

Deploying asymmetric systems that focus as much (if not more) on behaviors followed as outcomes achieved is not easy, and it requires a forward-thinking and active human resources department. Large professional services companies like The Boston Consulting Group demonstrate that such systems can be built at scale. And the investment is worth it, because such a system is a critical component of a culture of experimentation. After all, while people will *listen* when senior leaders implore people to innovate, they

---

lent book *The Signal and the Noise* that there is a chance—albeit slight—that a skilled poker player could play *ten thousand hands* and still lose money. Because most innovators generate only a handful of data points, it is even more important to look beyond the track record when assessing talent.

will *learn* what matters when they watch those who take risks that don't pan out get punished.

3. Project Disengagement Mechanisms That End the Plague of "Zombie Projects"

Senior leaders constantly report that their innovation efforts go too slowly or that they lack the resources to invest in innovative growth initiatives. One root problem is that the lack of an effective process to disengage from failed projects results in what I call *zombie projects*—walking undead that slowly shuffle along with limited prospects. Companies that stop the plague of zombie projects suddenly find they have many more resources than they realized and that the remaining projects suddenly accelerate.

Here's one way to demonstrate the impact of zombie projects. In the 1990s then Harvard Business School professors Steve Wheelwright and Kim Clark conducted research to look at the impact on productivity of splitting people across multiple projects. They asked engineers to estimate what percentage of their time was focused on value-added activities and what percentage was focused on non-value-added activities (planning meetings, preparing for planning meetings, preparing for meetings to prepare for planning meetings). In *Revolutionizing New Product Development*, they found that the time spent on value-added activities peaked at 80 percent when people worked on two projects. The percentage plummeted as engineers added more projects to their portfolio. An engineer split across five projects would spend 70 percent of his or her time on *nonproductive* activities.

Think about how you staff your new growth initiatives. If your company is like many others, it will ask people to spend a fraction of their time on a specific project. The theory is that dividing the work will help people go faster and get better results; the reality is there are many more things that need to get done than people anyway, so you need to do this in order to make progress. But how many successful start-up companies had part-time leaders? As the old saying goes, "You can't ask nine women to make a baby in a month."

What's behind all of this is appallingly poor mechanisms to shut down projects, even projects that in moments of honesty leaders would admit have little chance of moving the growth needle. Most companies treat the end of projects like the classic ending scene of the *Raiders of the Lost Ark*. Indiana Jones has been through hell and back to obtain the Ark of the Covenant, which allegedly contains the remains of the Ten Commandments. The Nazis' faces have melted, and all is right with the world. He gives the Ark to the US government. Does the government seek to study it? No. The last scene shows the Ark going into a massive warehouse filled with thousands of boxes. Clearly, the Ark will be buried with all of the other boxes, never to be opened again.

As thought leader Rita Gunther McGrath notes, there are two good things that can result from any innovation project: a great new product or business, or significant learning that can be applied within the organization. The second result too frequently gets treated like the Ark—a project that doesn't deliver against initial expectations quickly goes into a box, is put in the warehouse, and is never spoken of again. Managers race to move away from the "failure" as quickly as possible. This sets off all sorts of bad behaviors. High-potential managers begin to avoid working on seemingly risky projects because they believe they can embellish their resumes more effectively by working on sure things. The company starts prioritizing low-risk, low-return ideas that can't create meaningful growth. Zombie projects multiply because no one wants the scarlet "F" that comes from failure pinned to his or her resume. Worse, innovation teams working on doomed ideas can escalate resource commitments in hopes that they can somehow find a path out of a deepening hole. No one remembers that when you are deep in a hole, it might be time to stop shoveling.

Remember the reality: every idea is partially right and partially wrong. Missteps and course corrections are a core part of the innovation process. A seminal study in the mid-1980s found that many major new product innovation successes relied on lessons learned from historical failures. In fact, the authors found that the majority of the new product "failures" they studied were critical milestones that often presaged future successes. Typically, valuable insights came in the form of direct feedback about the viability of technology, consumer acceptance of features and pricing, as well as how to target new consumer segments and geographic markets.

The best companies seek to understand *why* they didn't deliver against their initial expectations. Perhaps there is an opportunity to change direction but still succeed. Or perhaps the initial expectations—which are often based on nothing more than educated guesses—were wrong, indicating a need to fine-tune the process by which initial expectations are calibrated. Maybe the company learned that the idea that looked so good on paper wasn't so good in reality. As long as that learning came without massive investment, a decision to stop a project and redirect resources in more promising directions should be celebrated.

Leaders play a critical role in encouraging this behavior by how they manage disengagement from projects, how they treat managers who work on commercial flops, and how they humanize the topic by describing their own failures. For example, Procter & Gamble chairman and CEO A. G. Lafley talks openly about his failures. "You learn far more from your failures than you do from your successes," he said at an innovation conference in 2008. "I can remember every time I struck out in high school baseball; I can remember every time I failed at P&G, and I failed a lot. Now, what we're trying to do now is fail a lot faster, fail a lot cheaper, so we can fail more and get onto the next idea or the next innovation that may become a commercial success. But failure is incredibly important, and learning from failure is very important." Another example of leader role modeling is noted entrepreneur Jeff Stibel, who created a "failure wall" in his company Dun & Bradstreet Credibility Corp. The wall combined memorable quotes about failure with personal examples describing individual failures and lessons learned. Stibel himself detailed three of his most memorable failures and signed his name to them. You don't get clearer signals from leadership than that!

Another key enabler is a portfolio mind-set. Remember, 75 percent of venture-backed companies fail to return capital to their investors. If a company's future hinges on a single idea, failure certainly can't be tolerated. A portfolio approach, on the other hand, recognizes the uncertainty in any given innovation effort. It means that a company should explore a handful of ideas for every success it seeks. A portfolio mind-set begins to remove the stigma that comes with failure, because not everything is expected to succeed. It also can lead to unanticipated outcomes as new opportunities to mash together different ideas emerge.

When you shut a project down, follow guidance laid out by McGrath for how to effectively disengage from projects: clearly spell out the reasons for stopping the project; create a plan to mitigate the impact on people who will be affected by the termination; and use a "symbolic event—a wake, a play, a memorial—to give people closure." Remember, you've saved your company from the plague of the zombie project, so pop some champagne!

Many think innovation is a purely creative act, but sometimes you have to destroy in order to create. Shutting projects down, extracting lessons learned, and celebrating that learning can be a critical innovation enabler.

4. Systems That Foster Connections to External Experts, Customers, and Employees

Over the last six decades, a number of scholars have studied the origins of breakthrough thinking. One common finding is that magic happens at intersections, when different backgrounds and different mind-sets collide. Companies should thus create systems that foster three categories of connections: connections to external experts, customers, and broad populations of employees. These kinds of connections help companies test assumptions quickly and tap into the world's best knowledge, regardless of where it lies.

1. Connections to External Experts

When companies are moving in new directions, by definition their internal staff lacks requisite domain expertise. The choice is to either spend years to develop that knowledge or follow the Newtonian path of "seeing further by standing on the shoulders of giants." Nothing stops someone inside a company from picking up the phone or pecking out an email to individually connect with an expert, but more formal programs can be helpful as well. One powerful way to connect to external experts is to create what is known as an *open innovation* program. The term traces back to a 2003 book by University of California professor Henry Chesbrough. Companies like Procter & Gamble, General Electric, and LEGO have found success by formalizing connections with individual inventors, university research programs, and more. Stefan Lindegaard's excellent 15inno network (www.15inno.com) provides useful guidance for setting up open innovation programs. Companies can consider two other ways of connecting with external experts:

- Participate in industry consortia or regularly send people to eclectic gatherings like the World Economic Forum meeting at Davos, the TED conference, or the SXSW festival in Dallas. These gatherings create opportunities for managers to receive stimulation and to build personal networks.
- Form relationships with venture capitalists who often have deep insight into emerging technologies and business models. It's easy to imagine win-win relationships where a company learns from the venture capitalists and gets a first peek at emerging technologies in exchange for giving the venture capitalists insight into the specifications of a business that would make an attractive acquisition target.

2. Connections to Customers

Steve Blank advises start-ups that they will find no answers inside the building. Because no business plan survives first contact with the market, companies need to ensure they have mechanisms that facilitate learning directly from customers. Consumer packaged goods companies (whose employees also happen to be potential customers) have a range of these mechanisms. For example, a nondescript warehouse about thirty minutes north of P&G's Cincinnati headquarters hosts the Home of the Future, where researchers can watch consumers try out new products. Many P&G offices have physical settings in which teams can share ideas with consumers or even learn to look at the world through the consumer's eyes. For example, the headquarters of P&G's baby-care business contains a room with oversized items so innovators have a toddler's perspective. P&G regularly tests new ideas by selling them outside corporate cafeterias or inside its employee store. Hindustan Unilever has a "street" in its headquarters in India where new-product teams pitch ideas to employees. Food companies regularly introduce new concepts into employee stores or even the corporate cafeteria; Anheuser-Busch InBev offices all have bars so employees can try out new concepts.

Companies in other industries can follow similar approaches. Imagine a telecommunications company that preidentifies a group of customers who agree to be beta testers of new offerings or creates a "network within a network" where it can test more sophisticated services without risking negative impact on its core communications network. In media, the New York Times Company launched beta620.nytimes.com, where consumers can play with ideas that aren't quite robust enough to make it onto the *Times*' main website. Exposing still-rough ideas to early feedback lets the *Times* accelerate the iterative process of disruptive discovery. When people have to work around systems to touch the marketplace, it makes experimentation that much harder.

3. Connections to Employees

In his 2005 book, *The Wisdom of Crowds*, James Surowiecki highlights the surprising finding that dispersed groups often outperform individual experts, even on complicated tasks like predicting the growth rate of the economy or the outcome of a presidential election. The year 2012 marked a maturation of the wisdom of crowds movement with Nate Silver's success in pooling together a diverse set of polls to crush individual experts' predictions in the US elections. Companies are beginning to get into the act as well, using so-called crowdsourcing techniques to tap into internal wisdom, wherever it might lie.

For example, in 2011 global financial powerhouse Citi rolled out Citi Ideas. Powered by software from Silicon Valley start-up Spigit, Citi Ideas enables groups within the organization to collaborate on problems in time-bounded "challenges" or on an ongoing basis. The technology gives employees permission to suggest new ideas, build on existing ideas, and rate the ideas of others. Incentives and gamelike aspects such as leader boards spark competitive engagement and encourage wide participation. Citi launched twenty-six campaigns in 2011 with more than thirty-five thousand people participating. In November 2011, Citi fielded its first global idea challenge to its 265,000 employees. More than twenty-three hundred ideas were generated and collaborated on by more than forty-five thousand people from thirteen business units and ninety-seven countries. Usage is accelerating with multiple business units within Citi signing up to run additional challenges as they see the speed, collaboration, and creativity enabled by ideation at scale.

Beyond generating individual ideas, internal connections can help with experiments by exposing hidden talents (recall the "T" discussion in chapter 5). Knowledge-intensive companies like consulting companies often create searchable online databases on internal social networks that help staff to quickly find the best people in the company on a particular topic.

First Mile–Friendly Systems in Action

Google and 3M are probably the most well documented examples of companies that have experimentation deep within their DNA. Both have systems that are consistent with those described in this chapter; notably, governance systems and incentives that support experimentation and ample internal and external connections. Other, less well-publicized organizations demonstrate the power of these systems in action as well.

The Palo Alto Research Center is known to the world by its four-letter abbreviation: PARC. Its hallowed halls gave birth to many of the underpinnings of the modern computing industry, including Ethernet, the graphical user interface, and the mouse (Steve Jobs was famously influenced by a trip to PARC in the late 1970s). Once Xerox's research laboratory, in 2002 it became a wholly owned subsidiary of the company, with its own profit and loss statement. After a failed effort to use licensing revenues to support research activities, in 2006 PARC became a contract research organization. Over the past few years, its scientists have conducted pathbreaking research in batteries, water clarification, and a number of other fields. Its new commercial focus has forced it to shift from applying scientific rigor only to its labs to bringing the same rigor to the entire innovation process. As Lawrence Lee (PARC's senior director of strategy) noted, "We ask our researchers to pursue research explorations by validating key technical uncertainties as quickly as possible. We ask our business development staff to create hypotheses for value proposition and validate them with clients early in order to inform the technical objectives and make sure we will create value if successful."

This conscious focus on experimentation doesn't occur just in the laboratories—it occurs in full view of the marketplace. Sophisticated portfolio management tools help PARC to make the right resource-allocation decisions between projects, and the organization's scientific roots mean that failure is understood as a necessary part of the process of discovery. For example, a PARC team was exploring a way to separate clean water from wastewater. By exploring a range of commercial applications, the team learned that finding a way to concentrate the "dirty" water actually had substantial commercial value. It received a $1 million grant from the California Energy Commission to commercialize technology that would help to generate methane.

Another company that has a deep culture of experimentation is W. L. Gore & Associates. Best known for its namesake Gore-Tex waterproof materials, the company has eight thousand employees (known as "associates") and forty-five manufacturing facilities, and participates in markets ranging from aerospace to venting products. The company has a uniquely decentralized culture, with relatively autonomous teams that self-form around specific opportunities. Experimentation—both in the labs and in the markets—is at the core of the culture. One way that Gore ensures that teams manage strategic risk appropriately is to build truly cross-functional teams. "Getting the team to actually decide what is the biggest uncertainty is quite fascinating," CEO Terri Kelly said during an Innosight leadership conference a few years ago. "You have to force marketing, product, and technical manufacturing to all be in the same room to tackle that. We spend a lot of time on getting the right team and empowering that team."

It might seem like self-forming teams would be a recipe for chaos, but Gore has two mechanisms to help ensure that the right resources flow to the right opportunities. First, a rigorous peer-review process ensures the best ideas get outsized resources. As Kelly notes, "There are healthy checks and balances." Gore regularly gives out a "sharpshooter" award to someone who "puts down" a project. Second, the company sets clear financial criteria that determine which business units and product lines it participates in. Cross the threshold, and you get investment capital. Fail to cross the threshold, and you get deprioritized, shut down, or spun out. The free-flowing nature and wide range of opportunities within Gore mean that it isn't a career killer to be part of a single failed project or latch on to a product line that gets shut down, though clearly it is good to avoid too many commercial failures!

Gore recognizes that it needs to approach resource allocation more fluidly, given the rapid pace of change in its markets. "The moment you do the forecast, it's wrong the next day. We all know that. But somehow we still convince ourselves that it is going to be more precise the one day of the year that we do budgeting," Kelly says. "You have to look deep into your systems to go in the opposite direction. Like your budgeting process. Your forecasting process. Your IT systems. They don't let you do quick experiments. You have to spend a lot more time on things that shouldn't be zapping the creativity, but they in fact are because they're all designed around high-speed processing."

PARC, Gore, 3M, Google, and more have reaped the benefits of building systems—combining appropriate governance, the right rewards, mechanisms for early and effective project disengagement, and substantial internal and external connections—that support structured experimentation. The final piece of the puzzle, the right leadership, is the subject of this book's final chapter.

Key Messages from This Chapter

1. Parallel project governance systems can pierce through the "fog of innovation."
2. Because innovation is unpredictable, rewards systems should focus on behaviors, not results.
3. Effective project disengagement mechanisms can help to stop the plague of "zombie projects."
4. As innovation occurs at intersections, companies should develop ways to foster internal and external connections.

CHAPTER 9

Leading in the First Mile

Almost seventy years ago, the great French poet Paul Valéry wrote "L'avenir est comme le reste: il n'est plus ce qu'il était," which roughly translates to "The future is not what it used to be." The line has never been more telling. Some of the statistics in the front of the book highlighted how fragile the business world is today. It is safe to assume that at least half of the world's twenty-five most admired companies will face some kind of significant struggle over the next decade. We are truly in an *age of discontinuity*, where the "new normal" is dealing with constant change.

Leaders a generation from now will have spent their working life in this era. Leaders two generations from now will have grown up in this era. They will naturally develop skills and coping mechanisms that allow them to handle some of the leadership challenges presented by never-ending change.

Today's leaders, however, face a different challenge. Many have spent a significant portion of their careers in far more stable environments. They carefully picked the right market segments, worked hard to develop competitive advantage, and then—through disciplined operations—milked it for years. They had to worry about competitors, of course, but could be reasonably sure that their competitors five years from now would be the same as today's competitors, who were largely the same as competitors five years ago (save, perhaps, for the latest entry from the low-cost country of the day, who was essentially picking off their least desirable customers anyway). As McGrath cogently noted in *The End of Competitive Advantage*, we are now in an era where companies have to learn how to exploit narrow windows of temporary competitive advantage: "The deeply ingrained structures and systems that executives rely on to extract maximum value from a competitive advantage are liabilities—outdated and even dangerous—in a fast-moving competitive environment."

Leaders inside large organizations have it particularly tough, because the ways in which they address these challenges *run counter* to what is required to successfully manage the core operations of a global multinational—that is, use multimodal approaches and encourage experimentation in the first mile and have focused systems that root out all uncertainty in your core business; build a performance-oriented culture and recognize that sometimes you want to give a hug to someone who just flopped; make decisions based on your experience sometimes and recognize that your experience is your greatest enemy other times.

The age of discontinuity is replete with paradox, where managers have to be able to approach problems from multiple frames and rise up to the challenge laid down by American author F. Scott Fitzgerald in his 1936 *Esquire* article: "The test of a first-rate intelligence is the ability to hold two opposed ideas in the mind at the same time and still retain the ability to function."

So what should a leader looking to develop the ability to confront paradox do? Consider three actions: seeking out chaos, diversifying your innovation cabinet, and developing nonrelated skills.

1. Seek Chaos

How can you tell whether you are short-listed to be an important person in an organization? One simple test is whether your span of control is increasing. Do you oversee more people? Do you touch more of the company's revenues? Size matters. But leaders in the future who need to deal with ambiguity have to reframe personal development opportunities. Instead of looking for bigger roles, seek out roles that are characterized by higher degrees of ambiguity. Consider moving to a new country to help open a branch office. Bonus points if that office is in an emerging market. Work on the launch of a new product or service line, even if sales projections are relatively low. Academics Jeff Dyer and Hal Gregersen note that their research into the behaviors followed by successful innovators shows that people who take expatriate assignments receive a statistical boost in their ability to innovate. At least one causal explanation is that being forced to re-create routines and find new ways to operate wires the brain to see hidden opportunities and learn by trial-and-error experimentation.

In 2009 an interesting opportunity opened up in Innosight. At the time I was the president of our core consulting business, working with our managing director and CEO to oversee a team of about forty people in the United States. The year 2008 had been choppy for us, but 2009 started positively, and we all felt good about our growth opportunities. A few years earlier, Innosight partner Brad Gambill had opened up a new office in Singapore. He turned that office into an outpost of business model experimentation. He first tried to develop an offering where we would build businesses "on demand" for large companies. In other words, an Innosight team would do all the work to build the foundation of a business and then sell it back to a company.[1] He then raised a small amount of capital so that we could incubate our own businesses. In early 2009 he reached agreement with the Singapore government on a novel deal structure that provided a very capital-efficient

1. This is a very hard model to make work, because the skills related to client management, business plan development, and entrepreneurial business building are quite different. Further, a standing team of generalists often lacks the required skills to really crack an industry-specific problem. Finally, sometimes a company choosing to completely outsource the creation of a venture is a good sign it isn't really that interested in a venture. Nonetheless, it was an interesting experiment, and we learned a lot from it.

way to do early-stage investment in start-up companies as well. In April 2009, however, he announced that he had received an exciting opportunity to lead strategy for LG Electronics and planned to leave Innosight. What to do? After talking it over with my colleagues and my wife, I decided to move to Singapore to pick up the incubation and investment side of our business. Even though the revenues and people under my control shrank significantly, the motivator for me was the chance to get a completely different set of experiences. I had to make strategic decisions about business lines, negotiate with lenders, determine a geographic strategy, prospect for consulting work in a new context, and explore what life was like as a venture capitalist. I made plenty of mistakes along the way but found that the rich set of experiences from operating in a new, uncertain environment provided a number of different operating frames that (I at least think) improved my ability to become a leader.[2]

You don't have to move to a foreign country to experience life on the edge. Consider something like taking a new role in your church or your children's school. The goal is to find a place where you are out of your comfort zone and forced to confront ambiguity more regularly. Through trial and error you will learn new skills that prepare you for the leadership challenges of the first mile.

---

2. Over time, we have deemphasized the incubation activities, redoubled our venture capital investment activities, and built a small team of consultants based in Singapore that provides advisory services to the regional arms of multinationals or indigenously based companies.

2. Diversify Your Innovation Cabinet

Doris Kearns Goodwin's *Team of Rivals* is an engaging biography of US president Abraham Lincoln. The book's title references how Lincoln—against all orthodoxy—picked people for his cabinet that had historically been his fierce rivals. His goal was to build the best team possible and seek as many differing opinions as possible. The diverse perspectives helped Lincoln make progress on issues that historically seemed impossible to overcome.

Similarly, consider the value of a *devil's advocate*. The term has a bum rap today, as it implies someone who argues for argument's sake and can always find the dark cloud in the silver lining. However, the term's historical legacy serves as a useful reminder of how a more diverse network can guide leaders through uncertain times. The term traces back to the sixteenth century, when Pope Sixtus V created a position where a lawyer would expressly create an argument *against* canonization. The basic idea was to ensure that a candidate that was eligible for sainthood met the highest possible bar. The role of the devil's advocate was to question. The person didn't necessarily have to *believe* the argument he was putting forward. Rather he had to argue a different perspective just to make sure there wasn't a critical area that had been overlooked. The role obviously had big impact. Between 1587 and its abolition in 1983, there were only about one hundred canonizations, or one roughly every four years. In the two decades that followed the position's abolition, roughly twenty-five candidates were canonized . . . per year!

Thought leader Roger Martin says that the key to addressing Fitzgerald's challenge is developing what he calls an *opposable mind.* As he notes, leaders with this skill can "without panicking or simply settling for one alterative or the other . . . produce a synthesis that is superior to either opposing idea. *Integrative thinking* is my term for . . . this discipline of consideration and synthesis—that is the hallmark of exceptional businesses and the people who run them."

One way to burnish this skill is to surround yourself with people who approach the world in different ways. Generally, we're inclined to network with people who look like us, went to the same schools as we did, or are in the same profession as we are. Those commonalities create connections that often prove powerful. However, leaders dealing with uncertainty need to make sure they have a diverse network that can provide unique perspectives on critical issues. Here's a simple test. Write down the twenty closest people in your professional network—people you consider close colleagues, mentors, or counselors. Count the number who:

- Have completely different academic degrees
- Have experience living on the edge, either as an artist or an entrepreneur
- Have spent a significant amount of time in a different country
- Work in a different industry

If the number is low, figure out ways to diversify your innovation cabinet. One simple way to do it is to find the *aliens* in your organization. Software entrepreneur Donna Auguste used this term when we worked together helping a newspaper company formulate new growth strategies. Auguste said the people at the fringes of the core business can often be the best sources for creative ideas. They don't quite fit the establishment, and that's exactly what you want. Hug your aliens! They can be a great source of nonobvious insight.

Another simple technique is simply to call up the most iconoclastic, weirdest person you know. Ask that person to introduce you to the most iconoclastic, weirdest person he or she knows. If it is you, you can have a short catch-up. Otherwise, odds are high that you'll create another intersection in your network.[3]

3. Pick Up New Skills

Calligraphy. Zen. Design. LSD. Say those four words to technology pundits, and an image of Apple founder Steve Jobs will pop into their heads. The legendary innovator's eclectic interests ended up being vital components of the dramatic growth he drove at Apple. For example, learning calligraphy during his brief time at Reed College wouldn't seem to be a particularly useful skill. However, when Jobs

3. This is one of the elements of "The Innovator's Pledge" that concludes *The Little Black Book of Innovation.*

was trying to determine ways to make the Macintosh computer line more distinctive, the calligraphy training led him to push for multiple typefaces and proportional fonts. It was but one component of making a computer—historically the province of hackers and hobbyists—friendly and approachable to laypeople.

On-the-job training traditionally focuses on providing hard and soft skills that improve a manager's near-term performance or somewhat longer-term leadership potential. Learning a new skill, particularly one disconnected from a leader's day-to-day role, would seem to be in good times a luxury, and in bad times a waste of time and money.

While developing disconnected skills might not provide an immediate return on investment, it does give leaders another frame that can improve integrative thinking. Developing disconnected skills provides other benefits. It can serve as a vehicle to make unique network connections. And, of course, it can provide a very positive source of energy to balance out the daily grind that occurs at even the most exciting of enterprises. And there can be unanticipated lessons from the effort.

For example, one of my colleagues decided that he was going to learn to play the guitar at the age of thirty-six. The only training program he could find near where he lived was with eight-year-olds. Unabashed, he signed up for the class. One side benefit of the training was that it reconnected to him to the unbridled creativity and joy that come from looking at the world through the eyes of a child. It also helped him nourish the humility that can help you be honest about what you really know during the early steps of the first mile. For the final performance of the class, where most of the children brought their thirtysomething fathers, my colleague brought his eight-year-old son.

Seeking chaos, hugging aliens, and learning to play the guitar might make some readers wonder whether there was an error at the digital printing plant, with a business book suddenly turning into a New Age self-help book. But new challenges require new approaches. Following the guidance in this chapter will help leaders deepen their ability to confront the challenges of the first mile and, more broadly, of leading businesses in a world where competitive advantage is increasingly a transient notion.

Key Messages from This Chapter

1. Leading in the first mile requires developing the ability to handle highly ambiguous, sometimes paradoxical problems.
2. Seeking chaos, diversifying networks, and developing disconnected skills are ways that leaders can improve their ability to confront these challenges.
3. Following this guidance has broader benefits—first mile challenges bear strong similarities to general challenges facing leaders in today's quickly changing world.

Parting Thoughts

There's no doubt that innovation is hard. It can be humbling when an idea that generated such enthusiasm during the planning stages ends up disappointing in the marketplace. Following the guidance in *The First Mile* should help readers at the very least approach innovation with more confidence by understanding what they can do to more scientifically manage its risks.

I offer six pieces of advice to end *The First Mile*.

1. **Be humble.** Any idea is going to be partially right and partially wrong. Even Steve Jobs didn't get it right all of the time! Humility helps to slay one of the biggest first mile enemies—the false confidence that comes from accepting an assumption as a fact.

2. **Be thorough.** Take the time to pick up your idea and look at it from multiple angles. Document your idea. Invest in desk research. Don't waste time learning something the world already knows.

3. **Be active.** Historical data has its limits. Learn in the market, with the market, and from the market.

4. **Be innovative.** What's your wind tunnel? There are lots of low-risk ways to test an idea. Remember to pick up the phone, run your own shrimp stress test, and build a MacGyver prototype.

5. **Be flexible.** Keep fixed commitments low to facilitate course correction as surprising results come in.

6. **Be integrative.** Innovation thrives at intersections, and diverse perspectives can be at least one way to avoid the cognitive biases that often cloud truth at the first mile.

And, above all else, *be bold.* The right actions can reduce risk, accelerate progress, and make innovation success attainable. Good luck in your efforts to pave innovation's first mile.

APPENDIX A

Innosight Ventures Assessment Tool

More details on the topics covered in any of these questions can be found in other Innosight books, notably *The Innovator's Guide to Growth*.

Assessment of the idea

Area	Poor fit	Average fit	Clear fit
Targets a job that is important to the customer	Customer doesn't care about the job—doesn't spend time or money trying to solve it	The job is a nagging pain point	The job is a "life level" need (even if the customer can't articulate it)
Customer faces a barrier inhibiting the ability to get the job done	No obvious barriers to getting the job done with today's offerings	Those with either wealth *or* skills can get the job done	Those with neither wealth nor skills can get the job done
The idea disrupts the status quo through simplicity, reliability, or affordability	The idea is a "better mousetrap"—more feature-rich than existing alternatives	The idea is a cheaper version of existing alternatives, achieved via a superior business model	The idea is simple, convenient, and cheap enough to enable the creation of new usage occasions/markets

(continued)

Assessment of the idea (*continued*)

Area	Poor fit	Average fit	Clear fit
The foothold customer can be described precisely	There is no identified foothold customer	The foothold customer can be "named" and described in detail	First sales have occurred
The expansion strategy involves many potential "hops" from the foothold	The expansion strategy is about completely penetrating the target customer segment	The expansion strategy involves expanding to new customers or contexts	The expansion strategy involves expanding to new "jobs to be done"
An attractive "size of prize story" is plausible	Everything has to go perfectly for the opportunity to be big	Many things have to go pretty well for the opportunity to be big	The "size of prize story" is obvious, with multiple paths to success
Competitive landscape has opportunities to build competitive advantage	The target market (and job) is populated with large, hungry competitors	Competitors would find it economically unattractive to respond	Early activities will be well off competitors' radar screens
The business model is well thought out and viable	Can't articulate business model	Clear *hypothesis* around business model	Early demonstrated proof of viable business model (at least at the unit level)
Cash flow characteristics allow early profitability to be a choice	Requires a large amount of investment and time to scale	Scaling will take time but requires manageable capital investment	Scaling can happen very quickly, making early profitability a choice
Relatively low technological uncertainty	Success requires "miracles"	Handful of manageable technological questions	No technology risk

Assessment of the management team

Area	Poor fit	Average fit	Clear fit
A plan is in place to test key assumptions in marketlike conditions	Major assumptions are not documented	Assumptions are identified but are difficult to test in the near term	Clear plan in place to learn about major assumptions in the next ninety days
Commitment and stamina to see the venture through	Not clear they are start-up-company material	Team appreciates what they are getting into and expresses commitment	Obvious they know what lies ahead and they have the "juice" to pull it off
Relevant experience	Lack experience in the field of the venture	Have relevant industry-sector experience or experience at another start up	The founders' experience is a strategic advantage
Critical mass on the management team	Existing team not sufficient to execute the first three months	Team can get through first six months but has gaps to be filled in	Team can handle all critical activities in next six months
Clear game plan	Major steps still need to be thought through	A project plan exists, but, as is typical for start-ups, it is probably optimistic and/or the team is in for some surprises and slips	High level of confidence that the team can hit their milestones

Path to profit

Area	Poor fit	Average fit	Clear fit
Multiple possible channels to reach foothold customers	The ability to get through an existing channel or to sell directly is not clear at the outset	Can see at the outset at least one receptive channel or the possibility of using direct sales to reach at least a portion of the target market	Direct sales possible and/or multiple channels that would profit from selling the product/service
It will be possible to get quality feedback from customers	Only path to market is through an indirect channel; customer contact not possible	Direct customer contact is possible	Easy to have direct customer relationships
Not dependent on technical or channel cooperation from industry players	One piece of a multipart solution; dependent on cooperation of other industry players	Some dependencies, but the venture has multiple options	Will sell a solution that cannot be blocked by interoperability issues or channel conflicts

APPENDIX B

Cognitive Biases and the First Mile

Navigating the first mile involves a scientific bent and a curious mind. Even the best minds, however, are subject to predictable biases that scientists argue are rooted in tens of thousands of years of evolution. Innovators facing the first mile ought to be aware of the following eight biases:

1. Planning fallacy: "Insiders" tend to do a poor job of estimating the time and cost of tasks. Corporations that are used to precision encounter endless frustrations when an innovator is consistently behind schedule and over budget.

2. Confirmation bias: In a noted experiment in the 1950s, a scientist showed a group of students from Princeton and Dartmouth footage from a controversial game between the two teams. Not surprisingly, the two groups saw the game very differently. Princeton students assumed that the Dartmouth team committed more fouls; Dartmouth students

assumed the opposite.[1] We have a tendency to seek out evidence that fits our preconceived notions and ignore evidence that doesn't. This bias is very dangerous for early-stage innovators, because it can lead you to miss signs that in hindsight suggested that a major course correction was required for success.

3. **The fundamental attribution error:** When something goes right, we tend to give extra credit to our own skills and brilliance; when things don't go right, we tend to blame things beyond our control. As the old saying goes, "Success has many fathers. Failure is an orphan." Honest assessments help us make more well-informed decisions about a business.

4. **The affect heuristic:** When we believe something is good, we tend to play up all of its good points and ignore or downplay all of its bad points. This heuristic—the confirmation bias's close cousin—often leads people working on an idea to come up with convoluted explanations for why negative data isn't really all that negative.

5. **The halo effect:** Edward Thorndike coined the term *halo effect* as a way to capture the fact that people who are attractive, personable, or good at a specific skill have a halo ascribed to them that makes

---

1. The Dartmouth viewers were correct, of course—at least, according to this Dartmouth alum.

reviewers assume they are good at everything. (Phil Rosenzweig's 2007 book by the same name shows how the concept hinders the usefulness of many business books.) The halo effect hampers the ability to form good first mile teams, because we overestimate the degree to which our "best" people will succeed in new circumstances.

6. Availability bias: We construct stories based on the data that is available, even if that story isn't correct. The danger comes when we draw conclusions from very small sample sizes. For example, you might go to a meeting and observe that everyone has placed an iPhone on the table. That must mean that Apple owns the global mobile phone market. While Apple does (as of the writing of this book) have a very strong competitive position, globally, Android-based devices outsell Apple devices, and in many emerging markets, devices manufactured by Nokia (which sold its mobile phone business to Microsoft in 2013) maintain a strong competitive position.

7. Anchoring bias: We overweight initial data. This bias has a particularly pernicious effect in large companies. Often, the only way to get approval for a new idea is to project overly inflated numbers. But, given the planning fallacy, those numbers usually take much longer to materialize than projected. When early results come in low, executives who

have anchored on big numbers can get disappointed and ax-happy.

8. Disaster neglect: When we run scenarios we don't consider true "black swan" events. So we think a downside scenario is a decrease of 10–20 percent in revenue, when there are scenarios that are much worse than this. This bias can lead innovators to miss some of the most critical risks in their business, what former US Defense Secretary Donald Rumsfeld famously called "unknown unknowns."

NOTES

PREFACE

Razor Rave experiment: Scott D. Anthony, *The Little Black Book of Innovation: How It Works, How to Do It* (Boston: Harvard Business Review Press, 2012), 184–187.

CHAPTER 1

Birth of Twitter: "How Twitter Was Born," http://www.140characters.com/2009/01/30/how-twitter-was-born/.

New product launch success rate: Scott D. Anthony, "The Planning Fallacy and the Innovator's Dilemma," HBR blog network, August 1, 2012, http://blogs.hbr.org/anthony/2012/08/the_planning_fallacy_and_the_i.html.

Percent of venture-backed start-ups that fail to return capital to investors: Deborah Gage, "The Venture Capital Secret: 3 Out of 4 Start-Ups Fail," *Wall Street Journal,* September 19, 2012, http://online.wsj.com/article/SB10000872396390443720204578004980476429190.html.

Percent of venture-backed software companies that achieve $1 billion valuations: Aileen Lee, "Welcome to the Unicorn Club: Learning from Billion-Dollar Startups," TechCrunch, November 2, 2013, http://techcrunch.com/2013/11/02/welcome-to-the-unicorn-club/.

Half-life of new companies: Scott Shane, *Illusions of Entrepreneurship: The Costly Myths That Entrepreneurs, Investors and Policy Makers Live By* (New Haven, CT: Yale University Press, 2008), figure 6.2, p. 99.

Thomas Edison's approach to developing the lightbulb: Mark W. Johnson and Josh Suskewicz, "How to Jump-Start the Clean Tech Economy," *Harvard Business Review,* November 2009, 52–60.

Chris Kimball background: Alex Halberstadt, "Cooking Isn't Creative, and It Isn't Easy," *New York Times Magazine,* October 11, 2012, http://www.nytimes.com/2012/10/14/magazine/cooks-illustrateds-christopher-kimball.html.

Statistical revolution in baseball: Alan Schwarz and Peter Gammons, *The Numbers Game: Baseball's Lifelong Fascination with Statistics* (New York: Thomas Dunne Books, 2003); Scott D. Anthony, "Major League Innovation," *Harvard Business Review,* October 2009, 51–54.

Seminal article on strategic uncertainty: Henry Mintzberg and James Waters, "Of Strategies, Deliberate and Emergent," *Strategic Management Journal* 6 (1985): 257.

McGrath and MacMillan book: Rita Gunther McGrath and Ian C. MacMillan, *Discovery-Driven Growth: A Breakthrough Process to Reduce Risk and Seize Opportunity* (Boston: Harvard Business Press, 2009).

Steve Blank on the difference between search *and* scale*:* Steven Gary Blank and Bob Dorf, *The Startup Owner's Manual: The Step-by-Step Guide for Building a Great Company* (Pescadero, CA: K&S Ranch, 2012).

Other useful reading: Eric Ries, *The Lean Startup: How Today's Entrepreneurs Use Continuous Innovation to Create Radically Successful Businesses* (New York: Crown Business, 2011) (see also http://www.startuplessonslearned.com/); Peter Sims, *Little Bets: How Breakthrough Ideas Emerge from Small Discoveries* (New York: Free Press, 2011).

Pertinent Innosight books: Scott D. Anthony and David S. Duncan, *Building a Growth Factory* (Boston: Harvard Business Review Press, 2012); Scott D. Anthony, Mark W. Johnson, Joseph V. Sinfield, and Elizabeth J. Altman, *The Innovator's Guide to Growth: Putting Disruptive Innovation to Work* (Boston: Harvard Business School Press, 2008).

CHAPTER 2

"Job to be done" concept: Clayton M. Christensen and Michael E. Raynor, *The Innovator's Solution: Creating and Sustaining Successful*

Growth (Boston: Harvard Business School Press, 2003), chapter 4; or Scott D. Anthony, *The Little Black Book of Innovation: How It Works, How to Do It* (Boston: Harvard Business Review Press, 2012), "Day 3" of Innovation Training.

CHAPTER 3

Academic research on backing a team versus backing an idea: Steven N. Kaplan, Berk A. Sensoy, and Per Stromberg, "Should Investors Bet on the Jockey or the Horse? Evidence from the Evolution of Firms from Early Business Plans to Public Companies," *Journal of Finance* 64, no. 1 (February 2009): 75–115.

Role of finance in innovation: Scott D. Anthony, "Innovation 3.0: How Finance Executives Can Help Spark an American Innovation Renaissance," *Financial Executive,* May 2012, http://www.financialexecutives.org/KenticoCMS/Financial-Executive-Magazine/2012_05/Innovation-3–0-%E2%80%93-Sparking-an-American-Renaissance.aspx#axzz2gRmoSFOe.

Business model innovation: Mark W. Johnson, *Seizing the White Space: Business Model Innovation for Growth and Renewal* (Boston: Harvard Business Press, 2010).

"All models are wrong, but some models are useful": George E. P. Box and Norman R. Draper, *Empirical Model-Building and Response Surfaces* (New York: Wiley, 1987), 424.

"For every one of our failures we had spreadsheets that looked awesome": Scott Cook, quoted in Jena McGregor, "How Failure Breeds Success," *BusinessWeek,* July 10, 2006.

4P model: Scott D. Anthony, "The 4 P's of Innovation," HBR blog network, June 10, 2010, http://blogs.hbr.org/anthony/2010/06/the_4ps_of_innovation.htm.

CHAPTER 4

Net Promoter Score: Frederick F. Reichheld, "The One Number You Need to Grow," *Harvard Business Review,* December 2003, 46–54.

Definition of deal killer and path dependency: Clark G. Gilbert and Matthew J. Eyring, "Beating the Odds When You Launch a New Venture," *Harvard Business Review,* May 2010, 92–98.

CHAPTER 5

US nuclear submarine program: Steven J. Spear, *The High-Velocity Edge: How Market Leaders Leverage Operational Excellence to Beat the Competition* (New York: McGraw-Hill, 2009); the book was originally published in 2008 under the name *Chasing the Rabbit.*

Value of learning in market: Scott D. Anthony, "Should You Back That Innovation Proposal?" HBR blog network, September 25, 2013, http://blogs.hbr.org/2013/09/should-you-back-that-innovation-proposal/.

Richard Wiseman's research on luck: Peter Sims, *Little Bets: How Breakthrough Ideas Emerge from Small Discoveries* (New York: Free Press, 2011); Scott D. Anthony, "The Dangers of Delegating Discovery," HBR blog network, September 23, 2011, http://blogs.hbr.org/anthony/2011/09/the_dangers_of_delegating_disc.html.

CHAPTER 6

Wilbur Wright's reflection on the wind tunnel: "The Wind Tunnel," http://www.countdowntokittyhawk.com/flyer/1903/wind_tunnel.html.

McDonald's "shrimp stress test": Janet Adamy, "For McDonald's, It's a Wrap," *Wall Street Journal,* January 30, 2007, http://online.wsj.com/article/SB117012746116291919.html.

Dow Corning Xiameter case study: Mark W. Johnson, *Seizing the White Space: Business Model Innovation for Growth and Renewal* (Boston: Harvard Business Press, 2010), 59.

Apollo 13 *rapid prototypes:* http://en.wikipedia.org/wiki/Apollo_13; see http://www.youtube.com/watch?v=Zm5nUEG5Bjo and http://www.youtube.com/watch?v=C2YZnTL596Q.

Tests I suggested to Michelle: Scott D. Anthony, "Nine Ways to Test an Entrepreneurial Idea," HBR blog network, March 11, 2011, http://

blogs.hbr.org/anthony/2011/03/60_minutes_to_a_more_innovativ .html.

Netflix history: Reed Hastings, as told to Amy Zipkin, "Out of Africa, Onto the Web," *New York Times,* December 17, 2006, http://www .nytimes.com/2006/12/17/jobs/17boss.html; Clark G. Gilbert and Matthew J. Eyring, "Beating the Odds When You Launch a New Venture," *Harvard Business Review,* May 2010, 92–98.

"Healthy Heart for All" story: Scott D. Anthony, "The New Corporate Garage," *Harvard Business Review,* September 2012, 44–53; and http:// www.innosight.com/impact-stories/Medtronic-Healthy-Heart-for -All-Innovation-Case-Study.cfm.

CHAPTER 7

Statistics on traffic fatalities caused by people shifting from flying to driving: James Ball, "September 11's Indirect Toll: Road Deaths Linked to Fearful Flyers," *The Guardian,* September 5, 2011.

ChoiceMed story: Clark G. Gilbert and Matthew J. Eyring, "Beating the Odds When You Launch a New Venture," *Harvard Business Review,* May 2010, 92–98.

Definition of planning fallacy: Daniel Kahneman and Amos Tversky, "Intuitive Prediction: Biases and Corrective Procedures," *TIMS Studies in Management Science* 12 (1979): 313–327; Daniel Kahnemann, *Thinking, Fast and Slow* (New York: Farrar, Strauss and Giroux, 2011). Scott D. Anthony, "The Planning Fallacy and the Innovator's Dilemma," HBR blog network, August 1, 2012, http//blogs.hbr.org/ anthony/2012/08/the_planning_fallacy_and_the_i.html.

Clayton Christensen's research on education: Clayton M. Christensen, Curtis W. Johnson, and Michael B. Horn, *Disrupting Class: How Disruptive Innovation Will Change the Way the World Learns* (New York: McGraw-Hill, 2008).

Schools of experience concept: Morgan McCall, *High Flyers: Developing the Next Generation of Leaders* (Boston: Harvard Business School Press, 1998).

Difference between discovery and delivery skills: Jeffrey Dyer, Hal Gregersen, and Clayton M. Christensen, *The Innovator's DNA: Mastering the Five Skills of Disruptive Innovators* (Boston: Harvard Business Review Press, 2011).

Dangers of premature scaling: Nathan Furr, "#1 Cause of Startup Death? Premature Scaling," *Forbes.com,* September 2, 2011, http://www.forbes.com/sites/nathanfurr/2011/09/02/1-cause-of-startup-death-premature-scaling/.

CHAPTER 8

The fog of innovation: Scott D. Anthony, "Seeing Through the Fog of Innovation," HBR blog network, February 25, 2013, http://blogs.hbr.org/anthony/2013/02/seeing_through_the_fog_of_inno.html.

Impact of grant review systems on researchers: Pierre Azoulay, Joshua S. Graff Zivin, and Gustavo Manso, "Incentives and Creativity: Evidence from the Academic Life Sciences," *RAND Journal of Economics* 42, no. 3 (2011): 527–554.

Tips for how to balance mistake minimizing and experiment encouraging approaches: Clark Gilbert, Matthew Eyring, and Richard N. Foster, "Two Routes to Resilience," *Harvard Business Review,* December 2012, 66–73; John Kotter, "Accelerate!" *Harvard Business Review,* November 2012, 44–58; Michael L. Tushman and Charles A. O'Reilly III, "The Ambidextrous Organization," *Harvard Business Review,* April 2004, 74–81.

Differentiating between luck and skill: Michael J. Mauboussin, *The Success Equation: Untangling Luck and Skill in Business, Sports, and Investing* (Boston: Harvard Business Review Press, 2012).

Blackjack example: Scott D. Anthony, *The Little Black Book of Innovation: How It Works, How to Do It* (Boston: Harvard Business Review Press, 2012), 230–235.

Asymmetric rewards: Gerard J. Tellis, *Unrelenting Innovation: How to Build a Culture for Marked Dominance* (San Francisco: John Wiley & Sons, 2013).

How failed projects lead to future success: M. A. Maidique and B. J. Zirger, "New Product Learning Cycle," *Research Policy* 14 (December 1985): 299–313.

Research on productivity losses from splitting resources across projects: Steven C. Wheelwright and Kim B. Clark, *Revolutionizing Product Development: Quantum Leaps in Speed, Efficiency and Quality* (New York: Free Press, 1992).

Rita McGrath's tips on project disengagement: Rita Gunther McGrath, "Failing by Design," *Harvard Business Review,* April 2011, 76–83.

A. G. Lafley on failure: Scott D. Anthony, "Game-Changing at Procter & Gamble," *Strategy & Innovation* 6, no. 4 (July–August 2008), www.innosight.com/documents/protected/SI/JulyAugust2008StrategyandInnovation.pdf; A. G. Lafley, interviewed by Karen Dillon, "I Think of My Failures as a Gift," *Harvard Business Review,* April 2011, 86–89.

Breakthroughs at the intersections: John Jewkes, David Sawers, and Richard Stillerman, *The Sources of Invention* (New York: St. Martin's Press, 1959); Frans Johansson, *The Medici Effect: What Elephants and Epidemics Can Teach Us About Innovation* (Boston: Harvard Business School Press, 2006); Steven Johnson, *Where Good Ideas Come From: The Natural History of Innovation* (New York: Riverhead Books, 2010); and Thomas Kuhn, *The Structure of Scientific Revolutions* (Chicago: University of Chicago Press, 1962).

Mechanisms to learn from customers: Scott D. Anthony and David S. Duncan, *Building a Growth Factory* (Boston: Harvard Business Review Press, 2012), sections on "Little Bets Labs" and "Idea Supply Chain."

Overview of PARC's innovation programs: Lawrence Lee, "Innovation as a Business: How to Create a Repeatable and Sustainable Innovation Engine," submission by PARC to McKinsey/*Harvard Business Review* innovation contest, January 7, 2013, http://www.mixprize.org/story/innovation-as-business.

CHAPTER 9

Rita McGrath's research on temporary competitive advantage: Rita Gunther McGrath, *The End of Competitive Advantage: How to Keep Your Strategy Moving as Fast as Your Business* (Boston: Harvard Business Review Press, 2013).

Other research on the increasing pace of change in today's world: Roger L. Martin, *The Opposable Mind: How Successful Leaders Win through Integrative Thinking* (Boston: Harvard Business School Press, 2007); Robert Kegan, *In Over Our Heads* (Cambridge, MA: Harvard University Press, 1994); Bob Johansen, *Leaders Make the Future* (San Francisco: Berrett-Koehler Publishers, 2009).

"The test of a first-rate intelligence . . .": F. Scott Fitzgerald, "The Crack-Up," *Esquire Magazine,* February 1936, http://www.esquire.com/features/the-crack-up.

Research on the benefit of expatriate assignments: Jeffrey Dyer, Hal Gregersen, and Clayton M. Christensen, *The Innovator's DNA: Mastering the Five Skills of Disruptive Innovators* (Boston: Harvard Business Review Press, 2011).

Quote on integrative thinking: Martin, *The Opposable Mind.*

KEY REFERENCES

Adner, Ron. *The Wide Lens: A New Strategy for Innovation.* New York: Penguin Group, 2012.

Anthony, Scott D. *The Little Black Book of Innovation: How It Works, How to Do It.* Boston: Harvard Business Review Press, 2012.

Anthony, Scott D., and David S. Duncan, *Building a Growth Factory.* Boston: Harvard Business Review Press, 2012.

Anthony, Scott D., Mark W. Johnson, Joseph V. Sinfield, and Elizabeth J. Altman. *The Innovator's Guide to Growth: Putting Disruptive Innovation to Work.* Boston: Harvard Business School Press, 2008.

Ariely, Dan. *Predictably Irrational: The Hidden Forces That Shape Our Decisions.* New York: Harper, 2008.

Azoulay, Pierre, Joshua S. Graff Zivin, and Gustavo Manso. "Incentives and Creativity: Evidence from the Academic Life Sciences." *RAND Journal of Economics* 42, no. 3 (2011): 527–554.

Blank, Steven Gary. *Four Steps to the Epiphany.* San Mateo, CA: Cafepress.com, 2005.

Blank, Steven Gary, and Bob Dorf. *The Startup Owner's Manual: The Step-by-Step Guide for Building a Great Company.* Pescadero, CA: K&S Ranch, 2012.

Brown, Tim. *Change by Design: How Design Thinking Transforms Organizations and Inspires Innovation.* New York: HarperCollins, 2009.

Christensen, Clayton M., and Michael E. Raynor, *The Innovator's Solution: Creating and Sustaining Successful Growth.* Boston: Harvard Business Review Press, 2013.

Duarte, Nancy, *Resonate: Present Visual Stories That Transform Audiences.* Hoboken, NJ: John Wiley & Sons, Inc., 2010.

Duhigg, Charles. *The Power of Habit: Why We Do What We Do in Life and Business.* New York: Random House, 2012.

Dyer, Jeffrey, Hal Gregersen, and Clayton M. Christensen. *The Innovator's DNA: Mastering the Five Skills of Disruptive Innovators.* Boston: Harvard Business Review Press, 2011.

Fried, Jason, and David Heinemeier Hansson. *Rework*. New York: Crown Business, 2010.

Gilbert, Clark G., and Matthew J. Eyring. "Beating the Odds When You Launch a New Venture," *Harvard Business Review,* May 2010, 92–98.

Gilbert, Clark G., Matthew Eyring, and Richard N. Foster. "Two Routes to Resilience." *Harvard Business Review,* December 2012, 66–73.

Johansson, Frans. *The Medici Effect: What Elephants and Epidemics Can Teach Us About Innovation.* Boston: Harvard Business School Press, 2006.

Johnson, Mark W. *Seizing the White Space: Business Model Innovation for Growth and Renewal.* Boston: Harvard Business Press, 2010.

Heath, Chip, and Dan Heath. *Switch: How to Change Things When Change Is Hard.* New York: Broadway Books, 2010.

Martin, Roger L. *The Opposable Mind: How Successful Leaders Win through Integrative Thinking.* Boston: Harvard Business School Press, 2007.

———. *The Design of Business: Why Design Thinking Is the Next Competitive Advantage.* Boston: Harvard Business Press, 2009.

Mauboussin, Michael J. *The Success Equation: Untangling Luck and Skill in Business, Sports, and Investing.* Boston: Harvard Business Review Press, 2012.

McCall, Morgan. *High Flyers: Developing the Next Generation of Leaders.* Boston: Harvard Business School Press, 1998.

McGrath, Rita Gunther. *The End of Competitive Advantage: How to Keep Your Strategy Moving as Fast as Your Business.* Boston: Harvard Business Review Press, 2013.

McGrath, Rita Gunther, and Ian C. MacMillan. "Discovery-Driven Planning," *Harvard Business Review,* July–August 1995, 44–54.

———. *Discovery-Driven Growth: A Breakthrough Process to Reduce Risk and Seize Opportunity.* Boston: Harvard Business Press, 2009.

Mintzberg, Henry, and James Waters. "Of Strategies, Deliberate and Emergent," *Strategic Management Journal* 6 (1985): 257.

Mullins, John, and Randy Komisar. *Getting to Plan B: Breaking through to a Better Business Model.* Boston: Harvard Business Press, 2009.

Reichheld, Frederick F. "The One Measure You Need to Grow," *Harvard Business Review,* December 2003, 46–54.

Ries, Eric. *The Lean Startup: How Today's Entrepreneurs Use Continuous Innovation to Create Radically Successful Businesses.* New York: Crown Business, 2011.

Rosenzweig, Philip. *The Halo Effect . . . and the Eight Other Business Delusions That Deceive Managers.* New York: Free Press, 2007.

Silver, Nate. *The Signal and the Noise: Why So Many Predictions Fail—But Some Don't.* New York: The Penguin Press, 2012.

Sims, Peter. *Little Bets: How Breakthrough Ideas Emerge from Small Discoveries.* New York: Free Press, 2011.

Spear, Steven J. *The High-Velocity Edge: How Market Leaders Leverage Operational Excellence to Beat the Competition.* New York: McGraw-Hill, 2009.

Taleb, Nassim Nicholas. *Antifragile: Things That Gain from Disorder.* New York: Random House, 2012.

Ulmer, David. *The Innovator's Extinction.* www.changeyourdna.com, 2013.

Watts, Duncan. *Everything Is Obvious**: How Common Sense Fails Us.* New York: Random House, 2012.

INDEX

ACKNOWLEDGMENTS

I consider myself extremely lucky. One primary reason is that I have had the privilege of learning from so many smart people.

From 2007 to 2009, a small group of people at Innosight, under the leadership of Brad Gambill, dedicated their lives to the hard work of incubating new businesses. Brad, Hari Nair, George Tattersfield, Alasdair Trotter, Kuen Loon Ho, Dheeraj Batra, Elnor Rozenrot, Dan Gay, and Vijay Raju in particular taught me an inordinate amount about what life is really like in innovation's first mile.

In 2005 Matt Eyring started exploring the possibility of using Innosight's IP as the backbone of an investment business. The baton was passed a few years ago to Pete Bonee and Piyush Chaplot, who drive those activities today. Matt, Pete, and Piyush have shown me how balancing careful analysis and a bias toward action helps to spot opportunities and shape winning businesses.

Building a business is incredibly tough, and the entrepreneurs we have funded, most notably Christoph Zrenner, Alvin Yap, Benjamin Duvall, Lux Anantharaman, Kal Takru, Jim Miller, Stephanie Chai, and Arrif Ziaudeen, have shown me how powerful the combination of grit, passion, and competence can be.

While innovation inside big companies often gets a bad rap, our corporate clients are no less a source of inspiration to me. I owe special thanks to Zia Zaman from SingTel, Bruce Brown from Procter & Gamble, and Keyne Monson and Dorothea Koh from Baxter, who each in their own way have helped me understand how to make large companies more conducive to strategic experimentation.

Field-based learning fortifies the academic backbone on which our work is based. Rita McGrath, Vijay Govindarajan, and Clayton Christensen in particular have been invaluable sources of wisdom as well as good friends over the past decade.

The team at Innosight teaches me something new every day. I owe particular gratitude to Mark Johnson. Mark and I have worked together for more than a decade now, and he has been unfailing in his support for the various paths I have chosen to explore and unwavering in his commitment to making Innosight a great company.

My colleagues and I also owe a substantial debt to our friends in Singapore—Teo Ming Kian, Bernard Nee, Francis Yeoh, CC Hang, Hau Koh Foo, Koh Boon Hwee, Bernard Siew, Low Teck Seng, SC Tien, and Tan Ka Huat—who have each provided critical support for our regional activities.

Longtime friends Karl Ronn, Clark Gilbert, Lib Gibson, David Goulait, and Michael Putz have provided never-ending sources of inspiration and insight. Lib in particular provided invaluable comments on an early, not-very-good version of the manuscript.

I'm also thankful for the long-term relationship we have with the team at Harvard Business Review Press, most particularly Tim Sullivan, Gardiner Morse, Andrea Ovans, Kevin Evers, Allison Peter, Julie Devoll, Sally Ashworth, and Stephani Finks.

Finally, the most important reason I consider myself lucky is that I have a simply amazing family. My parents, siblings, in-laws, nieces, nephews, aunts, and uncles are all treasures in their own way. Sorry we are so far away, but thanks for the constant love and support.

Joanne, I simply could not do what I do without you. You make me a better person, and I am thankful every day for the somewhat random chain of events that led to us meeting more than fifteen years ago. Charlie, Holly, and Harry, words can't describe how I feel when I open the door after a long trip and see the three of you rushing toward me with bright smiles on your faces. Keep growing up, of course, but don't ever change.

—Scott D. Anthony
On a conference call in Singapore to which
he should be paying more attention
November 2013

ABOUT THE AUTHOR

SCOTT D. ANTHONY is the managing partner of Innosight, a global management consulting and investment company that specializes in innovation. Based in the firm's Singapore office, Anthony has led its expansion into Asia-Pacific and its global venture capital investing activities (Innosight Ventures). He works with leading global companies to develop strategies and innovation capabilities for long-term, sustained growth.

Anthony's previous books are *Seeing What's Next: Using the Theories of Innovation to Predict Industry Change*; *The Innovator's Guide to Growth: Putting Disruptive Innovation to Work*; *The Silver Lining: An Innovation Playbook for Uncertain Times*; *The Little Black Book of Innovation: How It Works, How to Do It*; and *Building a Growth Factory.* He has written articles for publications including the *Wall Street Journal*, *Harvard Business Review*, *Bloomberg BusinessWeek*, *Fast Company*, *Forbes*, *Sloan Management Review*, *Advertising Age*, *Marketing Management*, and *Chief Executive.* He is on the board of directors of MediaCorp, a diversified media company based in Singapore. He has a regular column at Harvard Business Online (hbr.org), and his Twitter feed is @ScottDAnthony.

Anthony received a BA in economics, summa cum laude, from Dartmouth College and an MBA with high distinction from Harvard Business School, where he was a Baker Scholar. He lives in Singapore with his wife, Joanne, sons Charlie and Harry, and daughter Holly.